La Téléphonie and the Universal Musical Language

Books by David Whitwell

Philosophic Foundations of Education
Foundations of Music Education
Music Education of the Future
The Sousa Oral History Project
The Art of Musical Conducting
The Longy Club: 1900–1917
A Concise History of the Wind Band
Wagner on Bands
Berlioz on Bands
Chopin: A Self-Portrait
Aesthetics of Music in Ancient Civilizations
Aesthetics of Music in the Middle Ages
Aesthetics of Music in the Early Renaissance
Extraordinary Women

The History and Literature of the Wind Band and Wind Ensemble Series

Volume 1 The Wind Band and Wind Ensemble Before 1500
Volume 2 The Renaissance Wind Band and Wind Ensemble
Volume 3 The Baroque Wind Band and Wind Ensemble
Volume 4 The Wind Band and Wind Ensemble of the Classical Period (1750–1800)
Volume 5 The Nineteenth-Century Wind Band and Wind Ensemble
Volume 6 A Catalog of Multi-Part Repertoire for Wind Instruments or for Undesignated Instrumentation before 1600
Volume 7 Baroque Wind Band and Wind Ensemble Repertoire
Volume 8 Classical Period Wind Band and Wind Ensemble Repertoire
Volume 9 Nineteenth-Century Wind Band and Wind Ensemble Repertoire
Volume 10 A Supplementary Catalog of Wind Band and Wind Ensemble Repertoire
Volume 11 A Catalog of Wind Repertoire before the Twentieth Century for One to Five Players
Volume 12 A Second Supplementary Catalog of Early Wind Band and Wind Ensemble Repertoire
Volume 13 Name Index, Volumes 1–12, The History and Literature of the Wind Band and Wind Ensemble

www.whitwellbooks.com

David Whitwell

La Téléphonie and the Universal Musical Language

WHITWELL PUBLISHING • AUSTIN, TEXAS, USA

La Téléphonie and the Universal Musical Language
Second Edition
Dr. David Whitwell

WHITWELL PUBLISHING
815-A BRAZOS ST. #491
AUSTIN, TX 78701
WWW.WHITWELLPUBLISHING.COM

© 1995, 2012 by David Whitwell
All rights reserved. First edition 1995.
Second edition 2012

Composed in Bembo Book.
Published in the United States of America.
All images used in this book are in the public domain except where otherwise noted.

ISBN-13: 978-1-936512-41-6
ISBN-10: 1936512416

Cover image: 'Practicing the Musical Language,' a lithograph published by François Sudre, picturing a flutist and keyboard player 'communication,' while two other couples listen.

Contents

	Foreword	vii
	Sources	x
	Acknowledgements	xi
1	The Musical Language	1
2	La Téléphonie	11
3	The Universal Musical Language	37
4	After the Death of Sudre	67
	About The Author	73

Foreword

The long history of the use of a trumpet-type instrument for performing musical signals to control the movements of armies, or other large bodies of people, is widely documented in military accounts of Europe and before that in the ancient Greek literature, the Old Testament and in the tomb paintings of Egypt. The ancient Greek myth which attributes the origin of the trumpet to the sea god and his great conch carries the suggestion that this practice may be very remote (leaving aside the information in the Old Testament that God himself was a trumpet player).

The *Téléphonie* of Jean-François Sudre (1787–1862), which is described in Parisian newspapers between 1829 and 1864, might be thought of as the 'last chapter' of the military signal trumpet. By this we mean that, in the long history of trumpet signals, the *Téléphonie* was the last *new* idea, the last opportunity for the development of an entirely new phase in the use of trumpet signals. As it turned out, Sudre's new system never officially replaced the old traditional military trumpet signals, which continued to be used until they were finally retired by the telegraph, and more especially by radio, which was first called 'wireless,' in reference to the concept of a wireless telegraph.

The telegraph itself was in its first stage of development at the same time as the Téléphonie, and the two were often compared by military commissions studying them. In order, therefore, for the reader to appreciate the following accounts of the Téléphonie, it is perhaps appropriate to remind him what the telegraph was at this stage of its development.

The origins of the telegraph are found in the discoveries relative to the transmission of electricity, one of the most important contributors being Benjamin Franklin in 1745. The earliest prototype was suggested by an anonymous Scottish writer in 1753 in which twenty-six insulated wires were connected to something called a light ball above letters of the alphabet. With the invention of electromagnets, first applied to electric telegraphy by Ampère in 1820, small magnets placed on the receiving ends of 26 wires could be used to indicate the letters of the alphabet. Morse, of America, invented the concept of magneto-electric induction in 1831, and the Morse key in 1837. Interestingly enough, the famous Morse code was only developed in 1844 after one of his associates, Vail, made the discovery that dots and dashes could be distinguished by the difference in their *sound*.

However, the state of development of the telegraph by the time of François Sudre was a *visual* telegraph. The telegraph used by the French army at this time was a device set on a hill and was only of value to the soldiers who could see it during the daytime. Thus, when Sudre, the inventor of the *Téléphonie*, also referred to his invention as a '*Télégraphe Acoustique,*' he meant it was a 'telegraph' you could *hear*, as opposed to the other one which you could only *see*.

Sudre later indicated that it was the Institut de France, an institution which has always existed to reign supreme over the French language, who coined the term, *Téléphonie*. It was the very first appearance of one of the world's most familiar words.

Since this book discusses three separate inventions by Sudre, it might be helpful to the reader if we supply first a brief outline of the progress of his work. His initial invention was his Musical Language, which was a literal one letter per one note translation of French into music, using seven basic pitches. In order to make the Musical Language useful to the French military, it was necessary to accommodate his system to the military signal trumpet, the clarion, which was incapable of playing all the notes necessary for the Musical Language. Thus, his second invention, the *Téléphonie*, used only four pitches, *sol–do–mi–sol*, and in his final version only *three* pitches, *sol–do–sol*!

But now he was doing something fundamentally different: he was no longer literally transcribing words into music, but rather using musical sounds to *represent* phrases of language. This, in turn, led him to the idea of creating an international language through musical sounds. This was his third invention, one which he called the Universal Musical Language.

His idea, so beautiful in its concept of a global language based on music, was an entirely impractical one. This is nowhere more evident than in his great French dictionary of nearly 13,000 words represented by varying orders of the same two to four pitches. How could anyone ever learn to recognize by ear all these varieties of the same pitches? Musicians today know how difficult it is to recognize the various forms of a Tone Row in a serial composition, and modern clinical research suggests that our brain has very little success in hearing musical patterns when played backwards. While Schönberg insisted that a Tone Row beginning on a different pitch would be immediately recognized by the listener as the same Tone Row as the original, it is interesting to note that Sudre believed quite the contrary that a military signal could be kept secret from the enemy merely by transposing it to a different key!

In any event, in spite of his extraordinary public demonstrations of his new system of speaking through music, Sudre's discovery never resulted in something other people could use and, therefore, never earned him the recognition and financial rewards he believed were his due. In our view, however, all his years of work and sacrifice contributed to one great accomplishment. We believe it was from hearing Sudre's extraordinary public demonstrations in Paris that a fertile seed was planted in the mind of Richard Wagner, an idea which he transformed into his famous *leit-motiv* system.

At the heart of Sudre's Universal Musical Language is the proposition that the use of two, three or four notes could represent the abstract ideas, emotions, proper names, etc., of ordinary language. During the years 1830–1842 Sudre was giving public demonstrations of his new system in Paris, demonstrations received with astonishment by the public and which received extensive discussion in the most important newspapers and magazines dedicated to music. One private demonstration, described in an 1834 issue of the *Journal de Paris*, 'brought together the elite of the Parisian musical world.' Indeed a musical journal in Paris in 1835, *Le Pianiste*, seems to suggest that now everyone in Paris knew about this man and his work.

> All the world knows that this artist is the inventor of the musical language, a universal and precise language, and that the principles are of a simplicity and an irreproachable clarity …
>
> When it comes to posterity, that which M. Sudre already belongs to, we are assured that he will be most appreciated, and that, if we have elevated a statue of Gutenberg, the inventor of printing, we will find it just later to erect one to the inventor of the musical language.

Furthermore, six leading composers were actively engaged in the government's discussion of the idea: Cherubini, Lesuer, Berton, Boïeldieu, Auber and Paër. Berlioz, who of course was also present, was very interested in Sudre's new ideas and tried to help through his support.

It was during these very years that the young composer, Richard Wagner, was living in Paris. Given the great intellectual capacity of Wagner's mind, together with the fact that Paris was then only a city about the size of San Jose, California, it is impossible to think that all this went unnoticed by him. Although it would be another ten years before Wagner would actually begin constructing the music of his Ring operas on the basis of his so-called, *Leit-motifs*, one cannot help but notice that the fundamental principle is exactly the same principle which is the basis of Sudre's Universal Musical Language. Moreover, one is struck by the similarity of the manipulation of the musical fragments. Sudre, for example, points out his system includes,

> a peculiarity which does not exist in any other language, that is the possibility to express the inverse of the thought by the inverse of the symbol of that thought.

Sudre offers as an illustration, taken from his Universal Musical Language, the word, 'God,' which he represents by *do–mi–sol*, and 'Devil,' which he represents by *sol–mi–do*. This is, as anyone who has ever studied the 'Ring' knows, one of the techniques which Wagner also employs in the transformation of his motives.

While Wagner once mentioned that the name *Leitmotif,* was a suggestion of a young friend, he never discussed, in so far as we know, how the idea itself came to him. We believe the answer to this question will be clear once today's Wagner scholars become familiar with the long forgotten Sudre and his public demonstrations in Paris.

Sudre's innovative work met with public acclamations, but at the same time he met with a long series of disappointments in the failure of the government to follow their promises and encouragement with tangible recognition. Our greatest disappointment is that he did not live quite long enough to appreciate the fact that his great idea had taken root in one listener, Richard Wagner, and had blossomed into some of the world's greatest music.

Sources

The following materials are found under the shelf-marks indicated in the Music Division of the National Library of France, in Paris. My copies of these materials can be found in the Whitwell Archiv, *Bundesakademie für musikalische Jugendbildung*, in Trossingen, Germany. Also located in this archive is my copy of Sudre's *French Dictionary* containing some 13,000 words which can be expressed in his Universal Musical Language.

Sudre, Jean-François

> *Langue Musicale au moven de la quelle on peut converser sur tous les Instrumens.*
> Paris: Printed by the author, no date. L 8642
> > An autograph note, relative to this work, in the upper right-hand corner of the title page has been mysteriously torn off.
>
> ———. 40.B.624. Another copy.
>
> *Téléphonie ou Télégraphe Acoustique.* Paris: Imprimerie Royale, 1844. Recueil 150 (19)

Sudre, Joséphine

> *Langue Musicale Universelle inventée par François Sudre.* Paris: Printed by the author, 1866. 80.B.2826 [formerly: 21812]
> > Under this shelf-number are found a brief summary of her husband's work, his rules of syntax and his extensive dictionaries.

Compilations

> *Rapports sur La Langue Musicale invenée par M. F. Sudre.* Paris: Printed by the author, 1836. Recueil 91 (8).
> > Contains reprints of numerous newspaper reviews.
>
> *Langue Musicale ou Téléphonie, inventée par M. F. Sudre.* No publisher or date given. 80.B.2825
> > Contains reprints of two government reports and two *Institut de France* reports.
>
> *Rapport … Téléphonique …* Recueil 234 (9)

Acknowledgement

I am indebted to my friend and colleague, Craig Dabelstein, for his help in preparing this book for publication.

David Whitwell
Austin, Texas

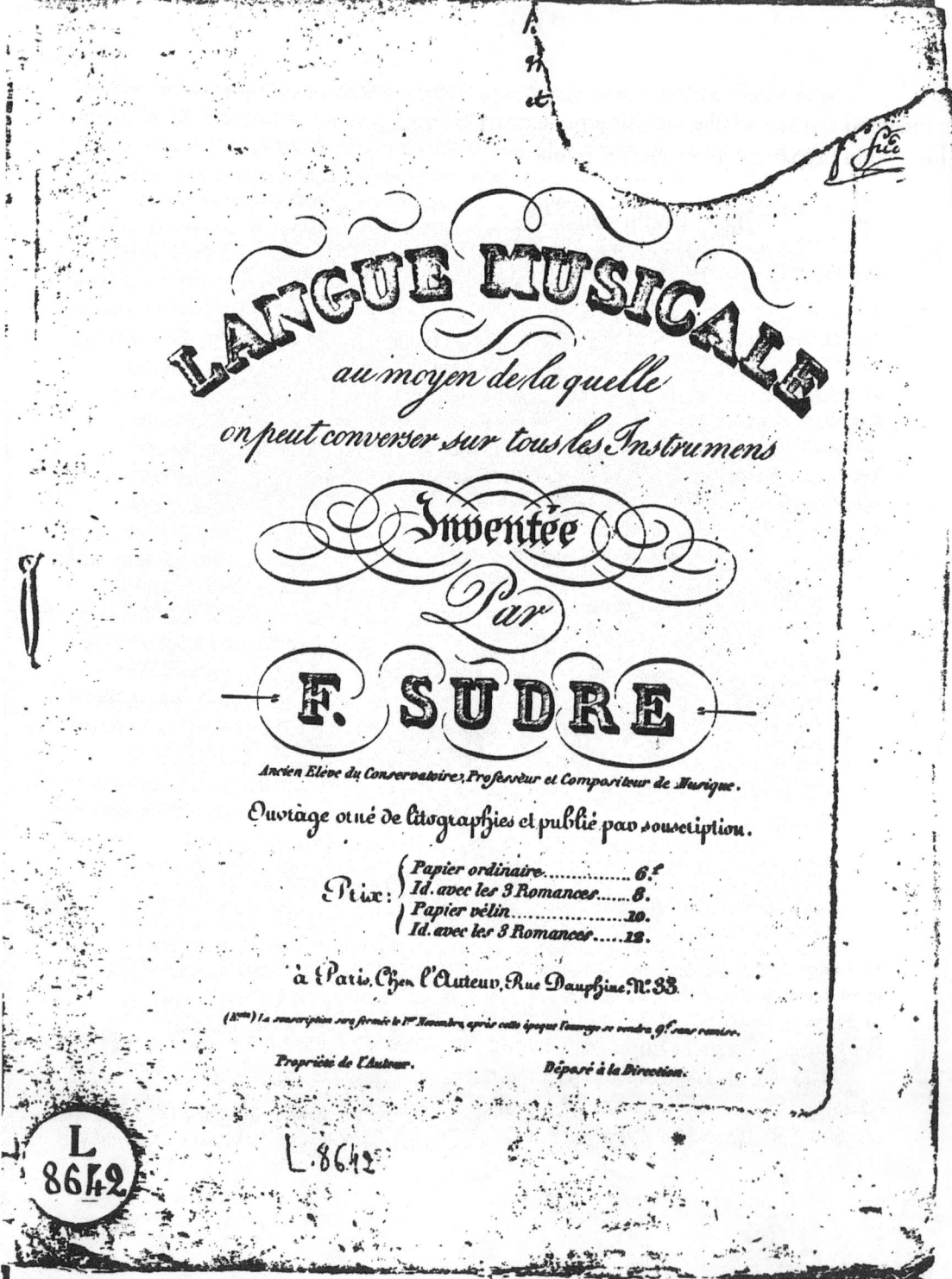

The Musical Language

Of the earliest years of François Sudre, we know only that he had attended the Paris Conservatoire, that he was a violinist and composer and that by 1817 he was a professor in 'the famous school of Soréze,' in the Department of Tarn. He was at this time finishing a music education method, the nature of which he only describes as 'the *simultaneous* teaching of music.' It is a pity that he chose not to leave more information on this new method, for, in hindsight, it may have been the most valuable of his various discoveries. In any case, the success of his new method of teaching music was such that it soon earned him a better position in Toulouse. Here he gave a public demonstration of this method and a review in the newspaper, *Moniteur universel*, of 21 July 1819, only strengthens our wish for more details of his method.

> The method of the mutual teaching of music, which Mr. Sudre has established in this city, obtained a success such as we might have expected from a professor who is as distinguished in his talent as in the purity of his taste.
>
> Last Sunday, Mr. Sudre gave new proof of the excellence of this method. In a demonstration, which was attended by the chief administrator of the Department, the president of the royal court and the mayor of Toulouse, we listened to this clever professor and a number of the students who attend his school, some of whom had had only a few months of lessons. It is impossible to do justice to this ensemble, the perfect accord of more than thirty young people while playing simultaneously multi-part lessons, which were improvised on-the-spot by their teacher.
>
> A large and varied audience demonstrated its admiration by repeated ovations.
>
> Since Mr. Sudre has introduced his excellent method and his charming compositions, groups of young people, all surprised to find themselves musicians, go through the streets playing wind ensemble compositions, with such togetherness and precision as the most experienced singers only obtain with difficulty.

The only remaining hint we have of what this novel music education system might have been, is found in the fact that during the next three years it transformed itself, in Sudre's mind, into his next invention, which he called the Musical Language.

The best information we have, regarding the transformation of the educational system into the Musical Language, comes from an article published in the Parisian newspaper, *Le Vouleur*, on 25 July 1835, which clearly was based on information supplied by Sudre himself. According to this article, Sudre had begun in 1817 to seek a 'musical alphabet' which would be both precise and simple to put into practice. The intellectual obstacles which he encountered at this time soon caused him to abandon the idea.

2   La Téléphonie and the Universal Musical Language

It was also at this time that Sudre met a brilliant young musician named Ernest Deldevez, who later would contribute so much to Sudre's public demonstrations. *Le Voleur* relates that one day, as Sudre was walking to his classes, he first saw Deldevez as a five-year-old child, standing near a water wagon and playing some 'little songs' on a small-size violin. Struck by the accuracy of the child's intonation, Sudre asked him who was his father.

'It is my son, Monsieur,' said a lady seated by the child's side.

'Who taught this child to play the violin?' asked Sudre.

'No one,' said the woman.

'But how did he learn how to tune his instrument?'

'By myself,' said the child.

'Let me see your violin,' demanded Sudre, whereupon he turned all the pegs, making every string out of tune. The child immediately retuned the instrument.

'But,' asked Sudre, 'who taught you all these little songs?' The mother explained that sometimes she would take him to the Vaudeville or the Variétés, where he learned the melodies by ear.

'Madame,' said Sudre, 'if this child belonged to me, in five or six years he would be my fortune!' Before separating, they exchanged addresses and promised to meet again in the future.

In 1822, Sudre returned to Paris for the purpose of studying operatic composition. It was at this time, according to this same newspaper, that he began to become obsessed with his new idea.

> Four years went by when one day, in returning to Paris, and nourishing himself without ceasing on his favorite idea, a subtle idea struck him, and he could yell like Archimedes: 'I found it!' In effect, his long patience had in an instant solved the problem he searched for. He [began writing out] his work, but in order to prove the results, he desired to encounter a young intelligence who could apply and prove the means of execution, that just until that day he had never tried but by himself.

He first discussed it in private with a musician he admired, one he identifies only as a musician 'intelligent and discreet,' who apparently encouraged him.

Next he sent for one of his better young students in Toulouse to come to Paris to be the first student of this new Musical Language. He tells us that after only fifteen lessons, with Sudre in his bedroom with his violin, and the student using the piano in the living room, they were able to carry on a conversation, posing and answering questions through music.

> One can imagine my contentment and satisfaction, hearing our ideas translated through an art that already exists in every place on earth and that not only excludes all difficulties in pronunciation, but national jealousies.
>
> How exciting and interesting it will be, trying to deduce the possible consequences from that ancient principle [music], which is as old as the world and will exist as long as there is science and nature.

Sudre now began to hold private demonstrations of his new Musical Language with his friends, who were in particular admiration when he allowed them to supply the sentences which he transmitted by playing his violin to his student in another room, who then translated them again into French. At one of these sessions a stenographer, named Chamrobert, employed by the *Moniteur universel*, was sufficiently impressed to mention the new system in the newspaper (29 October 1823).

> We recommend to young people who want to learn music, a new method by the inventor, M. Sudre. This professor has composed a *langage musical* through which two or more people can converse at a distance, either by their instruments or through their voices. The students, while enjoying themselves, will quickly learn to recognize pitch.
>
> Those who follow the lessons of M. Sudre, if they work with zeal and patience, will be assured of learning the art of music.

As planned, one year later, Ernest Deldevez arrived and became the student of Sudre and in 1825, he traveled various parts of France with Sudre, together with the young Charles Larsonneur, who was about the same age, giving demonstrations of the Musical Language. According to the *Le Voleur*, during this tour there was often a childish fight to see who would be the first to pronounce the correct words in response to Sudre's supplying the musical version on his violin.

At some point, giving his address in Paris as Dauphine, Nr. 32, Sudre paid out of his own funds to have published a brief method using his new system, under the title, *The Musical Language, a Means of Communication by all Instruments*. In this publication he quotes a passage by Voltaire (*Dictionnaire philosophique*) which he will use to demonstrate how language can be represented in his Musical Language. His choice of this quotation also reveals to us, moreover, that Sudre was already beginning to think of his later, and more grandiose, invention, the Universal Musical Language.

> There is no complete language which has the power to express all of our ideas and feelings, whose nuances are very numerous and imperceptible.
>
> No one can express precisely the degree of feeling that he feels. One is obliged, in consequence, to use a general name, such as love or hate, for thousands of different kinds of love and hate — everyone would be different. It is the same for pain and pleasure. All languages are imperfect, as we are …
>
> Languages have all been made successively [over time], and by degrees, according to our needs. It is the instinct common to all men which made the first grammar, without being aware of it. The Laplander, the Blacks, as well as the Greeks, needed to be able to express the past, present and future; and they did it, but not because they ever had meetings of logicians to create a language. No one ever created an absolutely regular language …
>
> Of all the languages of Europe, the French language must be the most general, because it is the most proper for conversation: its character is in common with the people who speak it …
>
> The most beautiful language should be the one which can express the weakest and most impetuous movements of the soul. It will be the one which most resembles music.

4 La Téléphonie and the Universal Musical Language

In describing his new Musical Language, Sudre first points out that each letter of the alphabet is represented by a single sound and by this means all words and ideas can be expressed. He admits that this kind of 'conversation' is very slow, but, on the other hand, he maintains it is superior to all other languages because it will project further than speech, 'up to 700 or 800 hundred feet if one uses a horn, clarinet, oboe, flute or violin.' He finds a further advantage in the fact that it can be written so quickly, consisting of only 'dots' [notes] and a staff of three lines. Indeed, he expresses the belief that this system will soon replace all other forms of stenography, or short-hand. He also devised a system of communicating the pitches by using the fingers of the hand, in order that the Musical Language could be used by the deaf.

He viewed his new system as one which every European could learn to recognize by ear, even if they knew nothing about music, providing the performer were accurate in his pitches.

Here is the 'musical alphabet' which lies at the heart of Sudre's initial Musical Language. In order to restrict himself to seven basic pitch symbols, some of the twenty-six alphabet letters are expressed as repeated pitches and some through the use a sharp sign before the pitch. In nineteenth-century French 'K' and 'W' were not used.

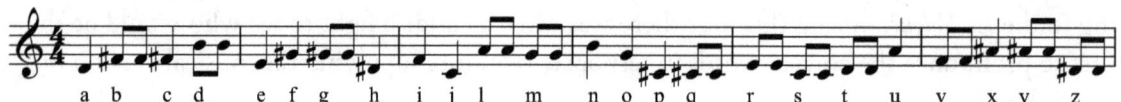

Sudre next illustrates how his new system conforms musically with the linguistic relationships of common French words.

Next Sudre recommends that one can make the Musical Language more like real music by employing freedom in rhythms and meter,

and by the employment of octave displacement.

He concludes these brief illustrations by presenting the Voltaire quotation, given previously, in his new Musical Language. We quote here the Musical Language portion for only the beginning words, 'There is no complete language.'

By 1827, four years later, Sudre was sufficiently confident in his new Musical Language to submit it to the Institut de France, the honorary body of artists, scientists and philosophers who must give approval before anything related to language can be considered truly 'French.' In order to accomplish this, he first requested of Henri Berton (1767–1844), a well-known Parisian composer at the time, permission to give him a private demonstration.

Berton invited Sudre to his home (Malaquais, 15) where eight or ten people were also in attendance. Sudre had taken along his eleven-year-old student, Ernest Deldevez, whom he locked in a room of Burton's house, and then invited the guests to supply a sentence. A M. Gail, a scholar of ancient Greece, wrote on a piece of paper, 'Women are roses, and that's it!' Sudre picked up his violin, played a sequence of notes, and then the young student opened the door 'and in a little voice,' said 'Women are roses, and that's it!' Several more demonstrations enjoyed the same success. Berton expressed his congratulations and promised to discuss the new Musical Language with the Academy of Fine Arts, of the Institut.

Fifteen days later, Sudre was invited to the Institut de France to demonstrate his system. Here, the marquis de Pastoret gave Sudre sentences in Greek and Latin, which Sudre played on his violin and his young student again returned the text of the original languages to the delight of everyone present.

This led to the appointment, in February 1828, of a nine-member commission, including five famous composers, of the Institut de France. Their report was published in the *Moniteur Universel* of 16 November 1828:

> Institut Royal de France
> Académie des Beaux-Arts
> Rapport sur la Langue Musicale
>
> Messieurs,
>   In your demonstration of last January 26 you have heard M. Sudre. He had the honor to develop the system of musical language, to speak with his violin, to write with musical notation and to have spontaneous translation made by his student, the young Deldevez, age 11. Several demonstrations were reiterated before you; all succeeded. The child always translated that which was transmitted musically by M. Sudre, and his translation was always confirmed by several of you who also dictated.

6 La Téléphonie and the Universal Musical Language

> The Academy has requested that the Music Section make a report on the works of M. Sudre. Your [Music] Section thinks it would also be useful, in any case, to include some distinguished members of the various academies which constitute the Institute. Your proposition has been put in effect and we are meeting on Monday, the 18th of this month, in the rooms of the Institut. This commission, composed of baron Fourier, Raoul-Rouchette, Cherubini, Lesueur, Berton, Catel and Boieldieu, after having made themselves familiar with all the preceding inventions of M. Sudre for the formation of his musical language, and after various demonstrations before us, recognized that the author has perfectly attained most of what he has proposed, that which we believe is a veritable musical language.
>
> The commission also thought that this system could offer an important service to society by offering men a new way of communicating their ideas over long distances, in the most profound obscurities. And especially in the art of war, the employment of this language could, in any case, be very useful to serve as the night telegraph (*télégraphe nocturne*), in the circumstances where often the military corps cannot communicate the orders necessary for the execution of such and such movements. Wind instruments could be very useful to employ this means, above all the small clarinet which every military band has. It is not only for the Staff level, but for [troops] all over France, for it has been demonstrated to us that in eight or ten lessons, if one is a musician, one can speak and write the language of M. Sudre. The translation, as we have seen before us by the young Deldevez, leads us to believe that this musical telegraph could be easily employed and useful in our military camps. The officer receives the order from his general, and it would then be transmitted from one part of the camp to another by the musicians of the corps. This demonstration was done last summer at midnight at the pont des Arts of the pont Royal, and it perfectly succeeded.
>
> We also believe we should assure the Academy that we believe it would be very easy, by means of transposition, to achieve a variety of [other uses for the] transmissions of this language, as for example use in the diplomatic correspondence where it would prevent the inconveniences which result for all the world's intelligences from transmission given in code symbols.
>
> The commission also believes that this new means of communication of thought could offer in other circumstances of life, a great advantage and the system of M. Sudre contains in all of it the germs of a ingenious and useful discovery.
>
> We have the honor to propose to you, Messieurs, that you accord your approbation to this report.
>
> Commission members:
> For the Académie des sciences: de Prony, Arago
> For the Académie française: baron Fourier
> For the Académie des inscriptions: Rochette
> For the Académie des Beaux-Arts: Chérubini, Lesueur, Berton, Catel and Boïeldieu

Following its quotation of this report, the newspaper observed that Sudre's musical language was indeed being studied by the military and then relates a demonstration which Sudre had also performed in the offices of the newspaper itself.

> We should, after having published this report, announce the truth of a special authorization under which various demonstrations by M. Sudre have been made in the presence of various general and superior officers, and that the means of rendering useful these applications are at this moment being studied with care.
>
> In regards to us, we should be permitted to make known a demonstration which was performed for us, and which has proved to us the dependability of the procedure of the transmission of ordinary language by translation into the musical language.

M. Sudre was presented to the bureau of the *Moniteur*, accompanied by a celebrated composer [Berton?], whose views we have read in the report of the Institut, and the young Deldevez. M. Sudre desired to give the editor a precise idea of his procedure. The young Deldevez was placed in another room and the editor wrote these words, 'Attaquez par la droite.' M. Sudre tuned his violin to a perfect C, and after a short interval, played various notes [translating the message into music]. The child translated these notes as 'attaquez' and, following successive notes, he translated 'par la droite.' The translation was exact and complete and numerous additional proofs could not prove a disadvantage. This should suffice to establish that M. Sudre has found an ingenious way to design by the notes of the scale, one or several letters of the alphabet and to convert the succession of these notes into a grammatical phrase. We recommend that it follow the application of the musical telegraph, and by these various demonstrations to establish the distance which the sound of the clarion [natural trumpet] could be heard and a way to voluntarily change the key or the symbols and to guarantee the exactness of the transmission by these responses. These diverse problems should be resolved in order to render useful, without being dangerous to the application, and M. Sudre seems certain to triumph over the difficulties which it presents.

Two days after the publication of the Institute report in the *Moniteur Universel*, another article in support of Sudre's Musical Language appeared in the *Figaro*.

De La Langue Musicale
Inventée par M. Sudre

We live in a time when everything in the progress of science is of interest to the public. The love of instruction and the taste of the fine arts is diffused to all classes of society; and if there is one study which is most general, it would certainly be music.

It is not surprising, then, that among the persons occupied by this sublime art, there would be found an artist who has managed, through all the combinations of sounds, to supply speech by instruments. But to *create* this new language, to give it clarity and precision, to render it overall universal, was an enterprise which presented huge difficulties to resolve. But since the Institut has declared that M. Sudre had perfectly attained the goal that he had proposed, it is not permitted to doubt that he has conquered it, and the musical language has all the characteristics we have mentioned.

The discovery of M. Sudre has already been given a place in numerous newspaper articles and has been the object of praise for the merits of the invention. But the different combinations which we mention as a priority has never before approached the work of M. Sudre.

The use of musical notes for secret correspondence is no longer a novelty and that includes the different code symbols used by diplomacy, or the letters to replace the numbers of the stores of our merchants. But the glory of the invention would stay entirely with M. Sudre, for we cannot prove that the results or any sort of results had been thought of or attained before him, by the same means or by any others.

The celebrated savants who have examined the procedures of this author, such as de Prony, Arago, Lesueur, Berton and Boïeldieu give M. Sudre justice and high praise. But the vote of these huge talents have been earned entirely by the ambition of the inventor. And the fruit of his goals — should it rest in the archives of the Institut? We do not think so; we engage ourselves strongly to press for the publication of these procedures, which as in all scientific enterprises, have need of the sanction of time, which only practice can lead to.

Sudre sent the report of the Institut, quoted above, to the Minister of War, in hopes of inspiring new interest on the part of the army in his new invention. The Minister sent the report to the Vicomte Decaux, president of the Committee of the General Staff of the army, who invited Sudre for an interview. This resulted in an invitation to Sudre to conduct some demonstrations at the royal school of the General Staff.

Here, before several general officers, Sudre invited one of them to give him a typical military order. He then played this on his violin, translating the order into his Musical Language, and it was repeated by an officer who played the string bass in another room. Sudre's student, with the officer, then transcribed the order back into French. Several demonstrations of this nature were done without mistake. Sudre adds that the officer repeating the musical form on his bass knew nothing of the meaning of the sounds he was playing. Sudre only wanted to demonstrate that by using an intermediary, one could communicate at longer distances.

The general Desprez was satisfied with this demonstration, but he was more interested in witnessing a demonstration of the Musical Language using the traditional natural trumpet, the clarion, which was used in the army, since he believed its sound would be easier to distinguish from far away. The problem for Sudre was that the clarion could not play all the notes necessary for his Musical Language. Thus, to fulfill this request, it was necessary for him to spend the following year creating an entirely new version of the Musical Language which used only four tones, *sol–ut–mi–sol*. It was this, his second invention, which would become known as the *Téléphonie*.

TÉLÉPHONIE
ou
TÉLÉGRAPHE ACOUSTIQUE
PRATIQUÉ AU MOYEN DE QUATRE SONS

sol   ut   mi   sol

EXÉCUTÉS SUR LE CLAIRON,

POUVANT, AU BESOIN, REMPLACER, LA NUIT COMME LE JOUR, TOUS LES MOYENS DE COMMUNICATION
DONT ON FAIT USAGE SUR TERRE AINSI QUE SUR MER,

INVENTÉ

Par F. SUDRE

ET APPROUVÉ

PAR L'INSTITUT ROYAL DE FRANCE

AINSI QUE PAR PLUSIEURS COMMISSIONS DE GÉNÉRAUX NOMMÉES PAR LE MINISTRE DE LA GUERRE.

———◆———

PARIS.
IMPRIMERIE ROYALE.
—
1844.

La Téléphonie

By December 1829, Sudre had transformed his Musical Language for seven pitches into the new system, which would soon become known as the *Téléphonie,* based on the four pitches, *sol–ut–mi–sol*, of the military clarion [natural trumpet]. He informed General Desprez who organized a trial on the Champ-de-Mars. Sudre, standing with his clarions by the École militaire, the military school which stands adjacent to the Champ-de-Mars, was asked to transmit orders by General Desprez to another General, Tholosé, who was standing on the Trocadéro hill. Some troops on horse, supplied by the commandant of the military school, were also positioned to relay the orders. The orders General Desprez selected were:

> Start to march at 4:00 in the morning.
> You will destroy the bridge at 6:00 A.M.
> The munitions are missing.
> The Division will go in the direction of Auteuil at 4:00 A.M.
> The river is overflowing.
> We hear a cannon coming from côté d'Issy.

General Desprez forwarded a favorable account of this demonstration to the Minister of War, who now appointed a formal commission for further study. This commission consisted of the generals, Comte de Durfort, Baron Corda, Baron Balthazard d'Arcy, Chevalier Nempde, Baron Marbot and Desprez, who presided. After further demonstrations with Sudre, this commission forwarded the following report to the Minister of War.

> Ministry of War
>
> The commission thinks that it is easy to use with advantage the musical language to make communication with troops of the same army which would be separated by a large river, a deep canyon, or that would occupy different points of a position, stable or far away, as well as to establish prompt communication between an army and an avant-garde which precedes it, or the rear garde which covers its retreat.
>
> We could also use it to direct the work of the bridge makers who are working on a large and rapid river.
>
> In several circumstances of our celebrated military annals, the musical language could have been very useful to our armies.
>
> For example, during the battle d'Essling, after our bridge on the Danube was destroyed, the staff general, placed on the island of Labau, was unable for several hours to give the order to the rest of the army to have a division sent immediately to Vienna, where one was afraid the population might begin to riot.
>
> The battle of Bussaco, in Portugal, when the attack of our troops had a very bad result because one of the divisions had its march stopped by a large trench and could not immediately alert the others, separated from it by the terrain of the mountains, even though they were able to hear the *instruments militaires*.

> Again, it was the difficulties of fast and direct communication in mountainous country that was the cause of the failure of the attack of our troops at Sorauren, in Spain, in 1813, when the French army was going to Pampelune to take it back from the English.
> In summary, the commission thinks that the method of M. Sudre will be useful only rarely, but in some very specific circumstances of war it will be very useful, which is enough to call for the favor of the government toward the inventor.

The presiding officer of the commission called upon Sudre to inquire what he desired from the government, proposing either one single payment in francs or, perhaps, the efforts of the Minister of War to persuade the Minister of the Interior to obtain for Sudre a professorship in the Conservatoire. Sudre responded that he would accept whatever they offered.

On 8 April 1829, Sudre received a personal letter of congratulations from the Minister of War, Vicomte Decaux.

> Monsieur,
>
> The commission of general officers, formed after the decision of last January 28, to examine the system of the musical language that you proposed for the possible use during war for the transmission of secret and rapid orders, reported to me on the demonstrations which you made before them.
>
> It seems to me, as a result of these demonstrations, as well as from the observations made by the commission, that in certain cases the use of this means of communication could be of great advantage, an advantage that, added to the simplicity of the means of its use, is enough to classify your method as a useful object.
>
> I can only congratulate you for creating this method of communication and thank you for offering it so kindly to the government of the king. I will honor you with a recommendation to the Minister of the Interior.

After a period of time elapsed, during which Sudre could see no specific plans underway by the army, he turned his attention to M. Hyde de Neuville, the Minister of the Navy. He directed Sudre to Toulon, where his system of communication could be tried both on shore and on the ocean.

A commission was formed by the administrator of the harbor in Toulon and the president of the commission, admiral Gallois, wrote the following report after the initial trials. It is in this report that we find the new term, *Téléphonie*, for the first time.

> Ministry of the Navy
>
> After a series of experiments made on different days on the shores of Toulon, and in different atmospheric circumstances more and less favorable, the commission is assured of the speed by which orders can be communicated by the method of the *Téléphonie* at a distance of 2,200 fathoms.
>
> For example, two minutes were sufficient to send, from the departure point to the point of reception, separated by a distance of 1,500 fathoms three orders taken from the book of signals.
>
> The different experiments confirmed the first judgment of the commission: they remarked that the wind had to be very intense for an admiral placed in the middle of his squadron not to be able to correspond with each single ship, since he could use the ships in between to relay his orders.

The commission adds that this means of communication is especially effective during the night, when the enemy is around, and we want to take him by surprise without using the fire signals which could compromise the army and give away its position.

But what especially attracted the attention of the commission was the advantage this *Téléphonique Méthod* will have in time of war when the army and navy have to communicate about strategic movements.

The commission thinks that employing the Téléphonie in the fog signals could extend the series of orders that one could give …

The commission agrees that this method offers a powerful addition to the means employed today by our squadrons to transmit their orders; one should take great consideration and one should quickly adopt it. It should be presented to a commission charged with studying the ways it might be adopted by the navy.

This report was then examined and discussed by a council of admirals, which recommended, through Admiral Missiessy, that the Minister should order that 'new experimentation should be done on shore and in the ocean to make sure what one could expect from the method of M. Sudre.'

The Minister, in addition to telling him of the finding of the council of admirals regarding the *Téléphonie*, sent him the following letter.

Monsieur,

As you know, I have charged a council of admirals to examine the report of the commission which attended you in the demonstration of your method which happened in Toulon under your supervision.

I have the honor to send you excerpts of the observations which I have received regarding this subject.

You will see that in its present state the *Téléphonie* could only be rarely used by the navy, however it seems appropriate that new experiments be made at sea and on shore.

I am ready to order new experiments, but I will do it only when I receive the assurance from yourself that you will improve the *Téléphonie* so that one can expect more satisfying results.

I know, Monsieur, that you are not trying to speculate on the invention of your method, but that you have the desire to be useful and the confidence I am offering to you here is proof that I appreciate your noble conduct.

Paris
December 3, 1829

Minister, Staff Secretariat of the Navy
Baron D'Haussez

On 4 September 1830, the journal, *Revue Musicale*, published the above army and naval reports, to which it added the following observations.

Langue Musicale de M. Sudre

We follow without doubt some details which we have given on the Musical Language discovered by M. Sudre, in the preceding volumes of the *Revue Musicale*. This language, destined primarily to establish, between the different corps of the army, or between the ships of the fleet, communications which are infinitely more rapid than those which result from ordinary means. Not having been satisfied with pointing out the perfection to which it would be susceptible, by very laudable perseverance

> M. Sudre has not stopped in his researches until he had resolved all the problems and conquered all the difficulties. The authentic reports which we have to this hour demonstrate that he has already arrived at a point in his work which has enriched the musical art with a veritable *téléphonie*.
>
> The possibility to communicate ideas made by diverse sounds has occupied various people for a century; but the results of researches on this subject never conformed to their theory, and we have been forced to conclude that the solution of the difficulties seemed insurmountable. M. Sudre was more brave or better advised than his predecessors. The mechanism of his musical language has remained his secret. In regard to the exterior forms, it consists of isolated sounds or couplets, which are transmitted closer and closer by means of a certain number of clarions. The result is a means of communication similar to that of the telegraph, and with a speed almost equal to that. But the Musical Language, with respect to that of the telegraph, has the advantage to be able to be put in usage overall, in the rugged places, in the seas, in positions between earth and water and the ability to be easily carried always by the generals or the captains of boats ...
>
> The evident results of these reports which we have come to read, is that the Musical Language of M. Sudre is not one of those imperfect inventions of which we speak for an instant and then quickly forget. It deserves to be classified among the useful discoveries.

During the next four years, Sudre worked at improving his *Téléphonie,* but he was also expanding his perspective for its possible use. Now he worked on making it applicable to the blind, deaf and mute, and it was also at this time that he began to formulate his grander Universal Musical Language, which we will discuss in the following chapter.

In early 1833 he submitted his improved *Téléphonie,* probably including the applications for the handicapped, once again to the Institut de France. We might assume that he believed another recommendation from this prestigious national institution might add political pressure on the military to adopt his system. In any case, it is clear that it was the military use which the Institute focused on and their lengthy report contains interesting comparisons between the *Téléphonie* and other communication devices then in use by the French armies. Here is the report the Institut made in September 1833.

> Institut Royal de France
>
> M. Sudre has presented to the Royal Academy of Fine Arts a system of Musical Language which was the object of a favorable report.
>
> Since then, he has been expanding and improving his work, which he recently submitted for the judgment of the Academy.
>
> In creating an artificial language, M. Sudre wanted to combine several advantages; he wanted to furnish a means of communication capable of expressing all our ideas; he wanted the new language to be susceptible to being rendered through sound, by characters or by gestures; that the system can be used nearby or transmit idea to distant locations; that it could be employed, as one wished, to communicate in the normal manner, or to establish a secret means of communication; finally, the system of sound would not be susceptible, as in the case of the pronunciation of spoken languages, to changes with the times, but by its nature will be unalterable.
>
> As you can see, gentlemen, M. Sudre has proposed the solution of a complicated problem, that he wanted to include all the conditions which have been separately proposed by authors of artificial languages who have occupied themselves with only the symbols, and appear among themselves so strongly opposed that they seem to nullify each other.

However, M. Sudre solved that problem and solved it in all its parts.

The commission, after a long analysis of the system in its philosophical aspect, recognizes, relative to the navy, the superiority of the Musical Language over the *megaphone*: because, as one knows, to use this kind of instrument [megaphone] it is necessary to articulate. All articulation is essentially problematic; only the vowels have force, [but] the consonants die easily at a short distance.

In using instruments, on the contrary, everything is in the manner of spoken vowels, consequently distinct and loud …

We have already talked about the advantage of the musical instruments which have a large intensity of sound, which are limited only by the creativity of the artists, in fact Nature, in this regard, imposes no limits, as one of the most distinguished physicians of the modern times has proven, who extended everyday the acoustic world. It will be worthless to replace the Musical Language, rather one would be looking to replace the human voice by an instrument, as one did by using the megaphone.

And what is remarkable is that not only does the superiority exist in their present state, but it is clear that they will eventually improve. This advantage should attract our attention to one of the applications of M. Sudre, especially if you can see how much potential some of its usages will have.

To be brief, one should first compare the system of M. Sudre to what is perfect in the other methods, that is to say the *Télégraphie* as it was invented by Chappe.

To design the analogous use of the Musical Language, we need an analogous name, that is why we presented the word *Téléphonie*: *sound* which one can hear from afar, as *Télégraphie* was designed for *writing* which can be seen from afar.

Because these two different arts are addressed to two different senses, their power will be necessarily characterized and limited by the nature of the senses, the milieu and the conditions in which one will use these two modes of communication.

First, sight and hearing are very different, in the way we are using them. Sight is incomparably larger, even limitless, because one can see distances which one cannot measure.

Hearing, in this regard, has an inferiority which no one can remedy; even if we are looking for some artistic way of helping the weakness of the hearing. But there is another inequality between the two senses, even if one uses one or the other of all the resources which science has made available.

If one compares the speed of light and sound, the superiority of light is extremely pronounced; the differences in speed, even if they are represented by numbers, are way beyond our imagination.

Sight has another advantage. The multiplicity of simultaneous impressions do not trouble its function, whereas with hearing one gets confused when several transmissions happen at the same time. [Another problem is] the variety of sounds, especially those we call noises, and we are not talking here about their intensity.

Finally, most people more easily perceive the differences between figures and colors, than the differences between sounds.

Therefore, anytime the sight can be used, with all of its advantages, the *Télégraphie* should prevail over the *Téléphonie*. These conditions are when the space is perfectly free, that is to say, from heights, where machines are employed whereby shape, size, color and mobility allows vision from a distance to perceive the multiplicity of signs.

But when the *Télégraphie* descends to the plains, it loses all the advantages it has from the heights.

Even if the curvature of the earth were uniform, soon the rays of light will render the signs invisible. But there are other difficulties, because in a plain, unless it is completely uncultivated and exists in short distances, the vision will be intercepted [by objects].

> Even in the case of a plain without vegetation, the unevenness will be an obstacle and it will be necessary to get up on a hill again to have all the conditions necessary for the superiority of the *Télégraphie*, that is to say, everything has to be premeditated, tried, adjusted in advance and with precision, that is to say, the use of the *Télégraphie* can not be improvised and it is absolutely impossible to use it in a lot of situations and weather conditions.
>
> Therefore it is from a fixed position and from a determined line of sight that the *Télégraphie* is better than any other method.
>
> Now we see that the *Téléphonie* is practical with advantage both on the plains or when the circumstances of use are unpredictable.
>
> The curvature of the earth, on a plain, will not stop the sound from being heard when the intensity is appropriate.
>
> It will be the same even in forests, uneven terrain, and the same with mountains, as long as they are not too large or too high, because sound can pass obstacles which are not too high or too wide.
>
> The proximity of the earth does not stop the propagation of the sound, on the contrary it is a favorable condition.
>
> It happens at daytime as well as at night, regardless of the transparency or opacity of the air.
>
> The *Téléphonie* can therefore be used on earth in most every single place, in night or day, without having to change the method. It is better at night because of the greater silence that reigns over the earth, better when the air is pure or when a hidden fog causes troubles.
>
> Therefore neither the diversity of the places or the unpredictable changes in the weather will stop the use of the *Téléphonie* on earth. Only one accidental circumstance can make it impractical: a loud and continuous noise. Even the wind, which diminishes its strength, cannot cancel it, even when the wind blows in direction contrary to the sound.
>
> The general application of this idea becomes stronger when we consider the instrument, which is simple and completely portable. It is always present in any circumstance when one could use it the most, and one learning it for other applications could easily learn to use it for this specific application, which is a condition of the highest importance for any practical application.
>
> Therefore, on earth, the *Télégraphie* is preferred when used in one line of sight, previously established on a hill.
>
> The *Téléphonie* is best in all situations where we have neither the time nor the choice of location …

Here the commission mentioned the favorable opinion of the general officers, charged by the Minister of War to examine this method, as well as the maritime commission under the Captain M. Gallois. The report continues:

> The multiplicity of theoretical and practical questions presented by the system of M. Sudre, and the importance of its applications concerning the State, required the careful attention of the commission; and it would not be possible to give a shorter report without being imprecise.
>
> We still have to study the conclusion of that report, before presenting it to the Academies' judgment.
>
> Regarding the theoretical part of the system, your commission's opinion is that the Musical Language invented by M. Sudre,
>
> 1. Offers a way of communication susceptible of expressing all our ideas;
> 2. It is susceptible to be communicated by sounds, by characters and by gestures;
> 3. It can be used either to communicate at short distances or to transmit ideas at a distance;
> 4. It can be used, as one wished, to communicate in the usual manner, or to establish a secret communication;

5. Finally, the systems of sounds is not susceptible, as the pronunciation of spoken languages is, to successive changes with time, but will remain by nature unalterable.

The commission is convinced of its utility for rapid communication to distant points.

The use of the Musical Language, compared to the use of the human voice, even aided by the megaphone, is much more intense.

Not only in its present state, but when it is more perfected it will be even better.

The *Téléphonie* can be employed in almost any situation and in almost any weather and it is the only practical solution when you are not on a high point or the preexistent conditions we discussed earlier.

These general applications take on a new value when one takes into consideration the fact that the instrument is as portable as possible; it is always present under any circumstances one wishes to use it, and where one is using it [as a musical instrument] for other purposes it can easily be used for this purpose [as a *Téléphonie*], a condition which is most important for any practical application.

The circumstances in which the *Téléphonie* seems to be the most useful is during the time of war, specifically related to the army.

In this regard, except for the conditions of height and established line [of sight], the *Téléphonie* is the sole practical [means of communication].

Its use has been confirmed by a commission of general and superior officers.

On the ocean, the *Téléphonie* has less carrying ability during the day than the [normal] signals, when one can use them.

But the signals can be used only to transmit orders which have been pre-established, the *Téléphonie* will supply the rest of the communication.

It must be used to augment the night signals, and even more the fog signals.

Finally our commission considered, on one hand, under the theoretical report, the extent and fruitful nature of the method of M. Sudre, founded on so simple a principle.

Seeing, on the other hand, the complete means of communicating rapidly to a distance, placed at the service of the State, brings honor to the country which has invented these two operations, your commission proposes to the Academy to give its approbation to the work of M. Sudre. And seeing with regret that the Academy has no possibility to recompense M. Sudre directly, the commission proposes that the Academy recommend him to the government.

Done at the Palace of the Institute, September 14, 1833.
Members of the Académie des Sciences: de Prony and de Freycinet
Member of the Académie française: Tissot
Members of the Académie des Inscriptions et Belles-Lettres: Comte de Laborde and Raoul-Rochette
Member of the Académie des Sciences morales et politiques: Edwards
Members of the Académie des Beaux-Arts: Chérubini, Lesueur, Berton, Boïeldieu, Auber and Paër

Although Sudre worked at making improvements in his *Téléphonie* in 1831–1833, there was no indication that either the army or the navy intended to make him a concrete proposal. Therefore, during this decade, Sudre's primary interest turned to developing his larger Universal Musical Language and traveling throughout France, Belgium, Germany and England giving public lectures and demonstrations of both his *Téléphonie* and Universal Musical Language. A number of articles and reviews of these public demonstrations survive, the first we have found being a description of one given before a select audience of musicians on 11 May 1834. The following day the *Journal de Paris* printed the following review.

> M. Sudre, the inventor of the musical language, has given yesterday in the rooms of M. Dietz, a demonstration where he brought together the elite of the Parisian musical world. There he exposed his ingenious system already honored by the vote of various commissions. First of all having converted a phonetic language into music, he dictates with the aid of his violin the words and phrases given by the public and then his student, placed in an adjoining room, instantly makes known [the original] to the entire assembly. But when going from the analysis to the synthesis, he makes the music into a true stenography, and transmits, with the aid of a clarion, by three very easy to appreciate sounds, entire words and entire phrases, then we must recognize that he has perfectly resolved a most difficult problem. Also every time the interpreter came to recite the dictation of the instrument, the listeners reacted lively with their astonishment and admiration! The immediate applications of this system to the art of the military and of the navy have been signaled in their diverse reports. We do not wish for a war for the great glory of M. Sudre; but, in the same manner that we melt down in times of peace the cannons which must serve in times of danger, in the same manner the *Téléphonie*, which could become a powerful arm, [has] a right to the encouragement of the authorities.

The following month, Sudre apparently asked to give a private demonstration for the editor of the Paris newspaper, *La Quotidienne*. The subsequent article, which appeared in the edition of 24 June 1834, includes an interesting insight into Sudre's original idea of the *Téléphonie*. Unlike the normal military trumpeter, who understood the relationship of what he played and the order it represented, in Sudre's concept the player might not know the military significance of what he played. The officer alone, for security, held the key.

> M. Sudre has always had the intention to create his musical system, the *Téléphonie*, for the communication of the army corps, in war as well as in peace. This miraculous language originated on his violin, with all of the known notes, modified according to the letters of the ordinary alphabet. It was necessary to reduce it in some way, that which his violin has already expressed with the force of art and science, to the most simple expression without removing its facility and richness, when he wanted to adapt it to the clarion which has only three notes. And M. Sudre has arrived at his goal.
>
> The demonstrations were done on the Champ-de-Mars, for the minister M. de Caux, in the presence of various general officers. I read the reports, and M. Sudre received the most sincere praise, and of the encouragement he had the right to be proud, because he had earned it. Near the military school, at the end of the Champ-de-Mars, two clarions performed the orders and in another place an officer wrote the orders as they were translated by a student of M. Sudre. This transcription, reported to the officer who commanded the school, was perfectly exact.
>
> So, suppose two battalions are divided by one or several enemy companies; it is necessary to turn these companies, to take another direction for reaching the woods or closest village. The clarion student of the first battalion would throw out to the wind the signal of correspondence, and his comrade of the second battalion would respond that he is attentive. Thereafter the orders are exchanged and the maneuver is executed, without the enemy knowing it and without being aware of any of the orders.
>
> Note that the clarion student would not need more than twelve lessons to be capable of corresponding exactly and never giving false notes. Furthermore, it is not the less advantageous that the clarion student would only write in symbols that which he comes to understand and repeat. He does not have the key of the symbols; only one or two officers would have the key. The clarion student is absolutely [nothing more than] one of the humans employed to pull on the wire the telegraph that would move an empire, without knowing the importance more or less of the movements of the huge arms of the machine. The clarion student could just as well replace a telegraph …

M. Sudre did not invent his system to surprise the intellectuals by tours de force which resembled magic; his aim was completely different. His was an extreme desire to be useful to his country, and to bring an immense improvement to the military service, with the drive of this iron will of genius, who had studied for so many years, who had fought against so many physical and moral obstacles, and who has finally come out victorious in this often desperate combat.

I had compared earlier the clarion students to the employees of the telegraph, and, in effect, the *Téléphonie* is another kind of telegraph.

M. Sudre took care of the inconveniences: from distance to distance he placed his clarion students in a broken line. The orders are constantly given and received, and the telegraph, after having translated into symbols, they bring to the capital, without losing any time, and with the same secrecy against those who would be interested to penetrate the mystery of these official communications.

We have spoken a lot of the night telegraph, in the essays we have done, which until now has presented huge difficulties. The *Téléphonie* offers the same advantages and does not present any of the obstacles that we have met in the first genre of transmission of orders or of news.

By night, in terms of the most obscure weather, in rain, fog and snow, the clarions are always heard: they speak always to the ears which take in easily the sounds of the symbols which the eyes cannot easily analyze when the lightest fog falls between two lantern telegraphs.

The clarions of M. Sudre can also render immense services to the sanitary lines and to the observation camps. It is over this point, principally, that the diverse commissions of general officers were named to examine this miraculous system.

The navy, which has nothing but the megaphone to transmit its orders, has also much to gain from this innovation in its service. We know the inevitable confusion of naval combat; when two squadrons are mixed the opposing flags are confusing to the eye, that the admiral finds himself separated from his satellites and when the cannons are firing from all of the port holes the megaphone becomes unuseful. It is a miracle that the maneuvers could be operated in a general and simultaneous manner. Each ship maneuvers on its own, obligated often not to worry the rest of the fleet. In contrast, the clarion students on each boat can transmit the orders almost without interruption, or at least each transmission would be one hundred times more active and more useful than the megaphone.

It is necessary to say, resting on this observation, that M. Sudre is at this moment working to perfect the clarion model whose sounds could be heard much further than the ordinary clarions. The ingenious perseverance of this savant make us believe that these new efforts will have a successful result.

And notice that this language, founded by this man who dreams only of the well-being of his country, does not have only one key, and we should not be afraid of the surprise on the part of the enemy. The key of the musical language could be changed each week: with a lot of work it could be changed each day, but that would be too scrupulous and unuseful. Besides, it would take years to disentangle the mystery that M. Sudre took twenty years to gain.

I had believed, like many others, that the alphabet of the musical language could be done by notes simply, by employing the different octaves and sharps and flats according to the necessity of the double vowels and consonants. M. Sudre easily demonstrated the silliness of this supposition. First of all the clarion has only three notes. And then the same execution that I heard convinced me of my error; M. Sudre and his students almost never changed the tone. I also read the symbols, with his instruction: each word of our vocabulary could be written at will on a staff of three or four lines. This should unbalance the smartest and the most incredulous.

In September 1834, Sudre traveled to Brussels for two demonstrations of his various inventions, including the *Téléphonie*. The first of these was given on 26 September in the Brussels Conservatory. The newspaper, *Le Lynx*, writing the following day reports that a military clarion was found at the last moment for the purposes of this demonstration.

> A clarion, brought one hour in advance from the barracks of Ste-Élisabeth, rendered the words and orders which we gave him to play; and they were interpreted without hesitation by [Sudre's student] M. Dancla, who was placed in an adjoining room.
> The viscomte de Pontécoulant had given the following military phrase:
> One hears the cannon at the cóte de St.-Cloud.
> Three notes on the clarion sufficed to transmit this.
> The twelve telegraphic symbols of M. Sudre prove how important it would be to simplify the signals of the visual telegraph, plus it could replace the 198 symbols of the government's telegraph, in order to render the sounds of all languages, as M. Sudre has already proved.
> We can see why the French commissioners of War and the Navy, in which general Després participated, have recognized and appreciated the importance of M. Sudre's system.

Within a few days the second demonstration was given in Brussels and on this occasion the audience included the Minister of War for Belgium.

> The Minister of War, who attended the demonstration, proposed to the author the transmission of several more or less complicated orders, and they were transmitted literally, with the rapidness of lightening, by the young Dancla. We recall, among others, the following order which was rendered by only three notes:
> Send us the cavalry.

When Sudre returned to France, in January 1835, he began to give a number of public demonstrations in Paris, in which he also included demonstrations of the *Téléphonie*. In his untiring efforts to interest the military in this means of communication, he had now apparently devised some means of combining the *Téléphonie* with the existing technology of the telegraph. This device is mentioned in the *Le National*, of 24 January 1835, which announced the first demonstration to be held in the Conservatory.

> A portable telegraph will be put in to use, by means of twelve symbols, to transmit by the sound of a clarion, by which this ingenious inventor will express all combinations of thought.

This new device was mentioned again in a review after this demonstration in the *Le Philantrope Universel*, 'Journal des Améliorations sociales,' for 5 February 1835.

> After this demonstration, M. Sudre made application to his *Téléphonie* system, especially intended for the art of war and the navy. A portable *télégraphe,* built especially for this demonstration, served to represent, by means of only twelve symbols, all the combinations of thought.

While most of the press attention during this period was addressed to the Universal Musical Language, one newspaper, the *Le Corsaire*, published in its issue of 16 February 1835, an article which was not a review, but simply a strong recommendation for the *Téléphonie* and its military possibilities. One wonders if history itself might have been altered, if Napoleon had had the *Téléphonie* at Waterloo!

> The musical language invented by M. Sudre, to which he had devoted a great number of years, and is truly worthy of serious attention, and we are surprised at the lack of concern by the government for an invention with such potential.
>
> I am not going into all the details of all the applications which one could make; it suffices only to say a few words regarding the important advantages which M. Sudre's *Téléphonie* would offer if employed by the army and navy. His method is simple and does not require any costs. It suffices to instruct an officer from the Staff Headquarters of each regiment, and to teach the trumpets for several weeks, in order to transmit the most secret orders of the general over all the line of the battle. Then, one would not have to send an envoy under fire, or aides-de-camp, or orders; and see how many brave young men would be saved, and at the same time your orders would arrive with more safety and their execution would be more prompt.
>
> Who knows how many of our unfortunate soldiers in Moscow, divided, followed, lost in foreign territory would have had their lives saved by the *Téléphonie* of M. Sudre. Who can say what would have happened at the Battle of Waterloo, if the division of Grouchy could have been warned.
>
> And don't tell me what I say [is a matter of chance]: the invention of M. Sudre has been examined by capable generals, by admirals, by commissions of the Royal Institut de France; all have been of unanimous opinion regarding the important results of many kinds we could obtain.
>
> We hope he will find among the Ministers some enlightened men, also friends of the nation, to examine, to appreciate this discovery, and, in any case to treat the inventor in a manner that would not discourage future inventors from tackling useful projects.

In the Summer of 1835, Sudre went to England for a demonstration of his discoveries in London. While most newspapers concentrated on the Universal Musical Language, the *Times*, of 10 July 1835, devoted most of its review to the *Téléphonie*. Included here is a very interesting anecdote regarding the atmosphere conditions which, in the opinion of the *Times*, remained a question which Sudre had not yet adequately resolved.

> The second part of this demonstration was concerned by experiments with his telegraphic invention which he called the *Téléphonie*. The advantage of this method of communication over the telegraph now in use, consists in the fact that the *Téléphonie* is not influenced by accidents of atmosphere or by local causes which intercept the view. The sound of a strong trumpet could reach the distance of three miles, the manner of communication could be transmitted for a distance of six miles in the space of ten minutes: that is to say, one third of the time employed by the present telegraph. Meanwhile, Mr. Sudre has not explained how the atmospheric obstacles could be vanquished by his mode of communication, and his mind must think on that point, so much more in the case of the daily experience where the smallest currents of air in a direction contrary to that of the sound, would stop the hearing at half a mile.
>
> All the world knows the anecdote of the sentinel who had been taken to court for having been found asleep at his post, at Windsor Castle, and then he proved he had been awake with the excuse that the clock of St. Paul had sounded thirteen times instead of twelve that night, in which the truth

was demonstrated. The soldier in question had probably been gifted with a rare portion of the acoustic faculty, and aided by an unusual tranquil atmosphere, in having discovered the irregularity of the clock of St. Paul on this particular occasion. But we doubt so much that this phenomenon, that the sound could arrive over such a great distance, would occur more than one time in five years.

> The author of this article can report one circumstance even more surprising regarding the progress of sounds when favored by the state of the atmosphere. One evening he was sitting by the window of his house in Europe, he heard during one hour the sounds of a violin which one plays in Asia. There is only one place in the world where this would be practical, and it is on the shores of the Bosphorus. The distance is a couple of miles and the same person occupied the same house during the following twelve months and someone played the violin every night on the opposite shore, but the sound of the instrument was never heard a second time.
>
> The telegraphic system of Mr. Sudre is nevertheless very ingenious and could be employed with great advantage for the transmissions of orders between corps of troops separated by great spaces.

In 1836 Sudre published a pamphlet containing a number of newspaper reviews of his discoveries. At the end of this publication, speaking in the third person, Sudre mentions that during his travels he had found a mechanical engineer who constructed a clarion-type instrument which could be heard at a distance of nine miles. It was one of the primary concerns of the military, how far the clarion, using Sudre's system, could be heard, thus it is unfortunate that he supplied here no further details.

In 1840, with the French conducting a war in Africa, Sudre decided to try once again to interest the military in his *Téléphonie*. He wrote to General Marbot, informing him of the improvements he had made in the *Téléphonie* since the last trials ten years earlier. Sudre received a replay from the general, dated 1 August 1840.

> Monsieur,
>
> I still remember perfectly in 1828 a commission, which I was a part of, charged by the Minister of War to examine the Musical Language, invented by you, which concluded that it would be useful in the army.
>
> You have now informed me that you have perfected your invention and you desire that I ask the royal Prince to adopt it for the army in Africa. I am convinced that it would be very useful in a lot of circumstances, especially for the troops which are in the mountainous part of the country; but I must remind you that only the Minister of War can order the adoption of anything related to the army, it is to him that you have to address your request.
>
> I have the honor, etc.
>
> Marbot

Perhaps the letter to General Marbot had some effect after all, for in 1841 suddenly both the army and the navy contacted Sudre requesting new demonstrations. Monsieur le Maréchal, the Minister of War, appointed a commission of general officers from all parts of the army to study the *Téléphonie* once again, and at the same time the Minister of the Navy ordered Sudre to go to Toulon for demonstrations with the fleet in the Mediterranean.

Poor Sudre, after a decade with no expression of interest, did not know which route he should pursue. Finally, he concluded that the naval squadron was more promising so he wrote General Schneider, who had been appointed president of the army commission, telling him of the naval orders and begging him to await his return.

Sudre departed for Toulon on 3 June 1841, for trials to be held on shore on the 6th and 9th of July. He was given seven clarions, taken from various ships, and after giving them some training, gave his demonstrations before a naval commission presided over by a M. Nonay, the captain of a ship. These trials resulted in the following report.

> The demonstrations made on shore in Toulon, on 6 and 9 July, have satisfied all the demands of the service for use in nice weather. It was necessary with a little wind, to have intermediaries to carry on the order in order to get to its destination. If the wind is too strong, as it often is in the port of Toulon, the sound will be limited to 200 meters, as found by the commission of 1829. Everyone knows that a big wind will even stop the sound of a cannon.
>
> The commission thinks that the clarion used does not present a sufficient intensity of sound and regrets that M. Sudre did not know of an instrument which would make his system perfectly usable. We understand that he is trying to find one. Otherwise the system will be incontestably of the greatest use by the navy.
>
> Finally, with the *clarion in Ut* which M. Sudre has adopted, it is evident that the system could render service to the fleet in a large number of circumstances.
>
> These demonstrations proved, as did the previous ones, that, in short, at night and in fog it could be of service to the officers and the clarions are familiar with the four notes employed. This study is very simple and M. Sudre was able to explain his system very quickly to some clarions whom he had seen for the first time.
>
> Regarding the use of the system of M. Sudre by the squadrons in the ocean, here the commission has some reservations and asks that this method will be used only after M. Sudre determines that the clarions and the persons in charge of the interpretation and transmission of the orders on board each ship are sufficiently educated and understand all the mechanisms of the *Téléphonie*, so that errors and confusion will not be attributed to the system.
>
> The commission expresses the unanimous opinion that the system of the *Téléphonie* of M. Sudre can be useful for the fleet; it is very important to experiment with it by squadrons on the ocean, because only there can one come to understand and appreciate exactly in which atmospheric circumstances, by night or in fog, one can use it or not use it.
>
> Made and written on board the ship Trident, on the shore of Toulon, July 19, 1841.
>
> MM. Mallet, de Grolier, de Mauléon. Lieutenants of the ship
> Nonay, Captain of the ship

Soon a squadron which was maneuvering off the isle of Corsica returned to Toulon and the Admiral Hugon, commanding officer, ordered Sudre to instruct thirty clarions belonging to the ships which composed the squadron. But shortly after the seventh lesson, the ships were ordered by the telegraph to go back to the sea. Sudre was very concerned that he should have to be responsible for the demonstrations when his clarions had received only half of their instruction, especially since it had been his experience that the naval clarions were given much less training in general that their colleagues in the army.

The fleet stopped near the island of Hydra, where the first trials occurred at 10:00 in the evening. The admiral gave several orders to be communicated to four ships of the light squadron. Sudre had organized the demonstration in such a way that the clarions aboard the several ships would repeat the order to assure the admiral that the message had been perfectly understood.

On the following day the squadron sailed in the direction of Africa and when they arrived off the coast of Algiers the admiral called for another demonstration. The ships were in the following formation, with Sudre on the *Trident* and the admiral on the *L'Océan*.

La Médée	Le Souverain	L'Océan	La Circé
	Le Jemmapes	L'Hercule	
	Le Suffren	Le Diadéme	
	Le Trident	Le Généreux	
	Le Scipon	L'Alger	
	L'Iéna	La Ville-de-Marseille	

The admiral now gave the following orders for Sudre to have his clarions transmit:

> Order to each ship to stay four hundred yards distance from the ship before them.
> The Admiral will signal the direction he wants to go: Northeast by 1/4th East.
> Order to proceed in two columns, wind in the back, in the natural order, the second squadron on the right follows the route previously signaled.
> Whatever the order the ships are organized, the second squadron is ordered to place itself on the left of the first one.
> The admiral alerts the ships that we will follow direction signals when we are out *of danger, when we pass an island or traverse a gulf.*

Finally, around 3:00 in the morning, a 'warning fanfare' was heard again from the admiral's ship, which transmitted to the fleet the following order:

> 4:00 A.M., North East.

The following day, at 8:00 A.M., the admiral wanted assurance that all of his night orders, communicated by Sudre's method, had been perfectly understood and ordered the ships to repeat the orders by their usual means of communication. When this operation was done, the admiral Hugon, using the marine telegraph, sent back the communication: '*Téléphonie* signals well done.'

When the fleet returned to Toulon, the commandant of the squadron named a new commission, which, after meeting several times, produced a report which concluded,

> Second Report Made to the Minister of the Navy
>
> During the time of night and fog, the signal *téléphonique* presents a definite advantage over the one now employed, since the application of those is extremely limited, and, by the means of the *Téléphonie* the admiral can send to one or several ships of his squadron all the orders which, on a very clear day, it will transmit to them by the means of little flags.

The *Téléphonie* presents, aside from everything else, the huge advantage during war times, in night or fog, of being able to communicate all necessary orders, near the enemy, with out the necessity of any signal fires, etc., which would reveal the presence of the fleet.

On the other hand, the commission thinks that at night, or in the fog, if the squadron were in disorder, following a calm, or another cause, the ships, not knowing in which order to repeat the *téléphonique* signals, it could be possible to have mistakes through the simultaneous repetition of several of them and the admiral could only with difficulty make sure that all the ships repeated the right signal.

After the debate finished, the president of the commission asked three questions.

First Question:
Does the system of M. Sudre have utility and application for the navy? The commission responded, yes, unanimously.

Second Question:
Is the clarion employed by M. Sudre sufficient? The commission responded, no, unanimously.

Third Question:
What conditions should the instrument fulfill to make the system of M. Sudre advantageous to the navy? The commission concluded:

1. The sound of the instrument should be as big as possible.
2. The emission of the sound should be easy to produce.
3. The diatonic intervals of their sounds must be such that there can be no error in the perception of these sounds.

M. le president, listening to the opinion of the commission, asked M. Sudre to come and asked him the following question: 'Do you believe it is possible to find the instrument needed'

Mr. Sudre answered that he was certain of it.

The commission, without wanting to impose an invariable rule, thought that for an instrument destined for use by the *Téléphonie* system, that human air might be replaced by an air compressor.

In the experiments which had been made on the ocean with the clarions, several had been successful, but not all of them.

Regarding this subject, M. Sudre observed to the commission that independent of the strength of the instrument, some of the experiments were not successful because the clarions did not receive the full training before going on the ships and once they embarked those on the ships they had no time to receive sufficient instruction.

In summary, the commission thinks that once the perfect instrument will be found, the system of transmissions of signals proposed by M. Sudre will be of great use to the fleet, in time of fog and at night.

The commission joins all the previous commissions in congratulating M. Sudre and thinks it is necessary to call for the most serious attention of the government to this invention.

Once the president made the report, he asked everyone on the commission if they approved all the opinions that were in the report; they all declared that they all agreed and had nothing else to add.

Done and written on the ship, Trident, August 20, 1841.

Sudre was somewhat disappointed with these demonstrations, in part because he was unable to provide sufficient training for the clarions. In fact, he found most of them could not even read music! He also complained that some of the ships were not in their proper positions and one, the *Ville-de-Marseille*, was so far off course it could not participate at all. His experience made him all the more aware how important the planning for his demonstrations was, but, at the same time, he realized it was a rare opportunity for him to actually try his system at sea.

Upon his return to Paris, Sudre went to see General Schneider, who organized the demonstration for the army commission. Sudre was now given twenty clarions which he chose from the 5th, 10th and 50th regiments encamped in Montreuil, Romainville and Fontenay-sous-Bois.

These demonstrations were again held on the Champ-de-Mars and Sudre attributed his success not only to the fact that he had sufficient time to train the clarions, but also 'because they already knew the four notes, *sol, ut, me, sol*, and if necessary they could write them.'

The commission wrote a detailed report which was addressed to M. le Maréchal, Minister of War, and reached the following conclusions:

> The *Téléphonie* is one of a number of these inventions, being based on a very simple principle, which still needs experimentation to convince us of their utility and possible applications advantageous to a special service. Your commission thinks that for the goal it has to fulfill, that it must organize a series of experiments specifically designed to make sure that this means of communication satisfies the conditions which are necessary to transmit prompt and secret orders for long distances.
>
> Consequently, after hearing M. Sudre explain the theory of his system and explain how easy it was to train an intelligent person to understand the Musical Language, and to arrange promptly for the clarions of the regiment to transmit the sounds of the *Téléphonie*, our commission organized a grand demonstration on the Champ-de-Mars.
>
> Twenty infantry clarions, placed at the disposal of M. Sudre, had to execute the transmissions after instruction in 15 or 20 lessons.
>
> For the purpose of the demonstration, they were divided into three mobile divisions, the first one stayed with the commission, and each of the divisions went to their respective positions, as indicated by the signal given by M. Sudre, who demonstrated that by giving regulated signals one could order or interrogate at a distance any of those divisions, without the others answering, even if they heard the same signal.
>
> During these demonstrations, the repetition of the *Téléphonie* sounds of the transmitted orders came back from the division the commission wanted to interrogate.
>
> A person who understood the Musical Language was placed in a location within the Champ-de-Mars, to translate, in normal language, each *Téléphonie* message as soon as the transmission was made by the respective clarions. This made the results immediately available to the commission, which was generally satisfied with the demonstrations, in which previously prepared, and extemporaneous, orders had been transmitted. An order which contained names of places was also transmitted faithfully.
>
> In another demonstration, bearing on a request by the Minister of War, the commission made a new test of the communication by the *Téléphonie*, using improvised orders, using proper names. We wanted to see how easy it was to translate the Musical Language into ordinary language, and visa versa.
>
> All of these experiments were a complete success.
>
> Finally, the commission wanted M. Sudre to demonstrate, through a practical example, that the method would be easy to learn. So an artillery officer, a member of the commission was selected, who received a lesson of only 45 minutes, to see if he could translate into ordinary language a communication either written in the Musical Language or played by the clarion.
>
> Three demonstrations of the *Téléphonie* communication happened in this session: the first was a standard order, one was an improvised order, and the third was a transmission done with changing the key of the symbols.
>
> This infantry officer, in each of the demonstrations, gave without hesitation the exact translation in ordinary language of the message transmitted by the clarion.

After these last experiments, M. le Maréchal and the commission were sufficiently enlightened by the system of correspondence invented by M. Sudre.

The system is completely acoustic based, that is to say, sound in all of its purity, which makes the method simple, clear and easy in its application.

It is executed by the clarion, using four sounds, separated by large intervals which makes the perception easy, even for the person who has no understanding of music.

By making some improvements in his method, M. Sudre made it similar to the *télégraphe* of the government, by giving it the possibility to express *all ideas*, including proper names and names of towns.

To be sure of the transmission of the sounds, the same sounds will be returned in the same way using the clarion.

If there is any mistake in this repetition of the sound, the clarion which originally transmitted the sound will give the correspondent a 'warning fanfare,' and repeat immediately the original sounds which had not been repeated faithfully.

In this *acoustic téléphonie*, as well as in the *visual télégraphie*, except for the established signals, the clarions had no understanding of the meaning of the sounds they were transmitting.

Finally, the possibility of being able to change the key of the symbols, guarantees the secrecy of the messages.

Following this examination, the special commission informed M. le Maréchal that this system of correspondence:

> Could be used with advantage in the ordinary service of troops, as well as in the operations of an army in campaign.
>
> That this means of communication is easy to execute for the soldiers which have to transmit acoustic signals, and much easier for the officer in charge of interpreting them.
>
> If adopted for the army, doesn't require specific training, nor a specific machine, since the men and the instrument are already existing the regiments.

The special commission has the honor to ask for your approval, M. le Maréchal, of the following propositions.

1. That the system of correspondence invented by M. Sudre is practical for the service of the army.
2. A school of Téléphonie, with the object of teaching the method of communication by all the clarions of the regiments, should be created under the direction of M. Sudre. If this school could be established at the École-Militaire, the proximity of the Champ-de-Mars offers great facility for the exercises of the clarions.
3. We should give to M. Sudre, the inventor of the Musical Language and of the *Téléphonie*, a recompense of the same nature as those given authors of important discoveries, for their relinquishment of their invention to the government. This compensation is legitimately deserved by M. Sudre, who during long years has consecrated his time, his life, as well as his fortune, to perfect this invention for the honor of France.

Paris February 28, 1843
MM. Generals Schneider, president
de Lawoestine
Marquis de la Place
Baron Daullé
Colonel Coraboeuf

The Minister of War, apparently satisfied with this trial of the *Téléphonie*, now turned his attention to the problem of the necessary training which would be required if this system were adopted to replace the traditional clarion signals of the army. Therefore, he appointed yet another commission, consisting of Generals Schneider, Baron Marbot, Baron Duchand, Marquis de Lawoestine and Maréchal de Bellonnet, to whom he addressed four specific questions.

After additional demonstrations by Sudre, the commission wrote the following report:

M. le Maréchal,

The commission you created by your orders of April 20 and May 6, was to examine the most advantageous means of making it possible for all the army corps to correspond with the *Téléphonie* method invented by M. Sudre. The commission wanted to answer quickly all the questions you have addressed to it.

The commission read with attention the report which you made on February 28 and sent to be read.

This report summarizes the work of numerous commissions who over the past 15 years have studied the method of M. Sudre and his improvements.

All had recognized that this method could be useful in the army, and in all the corps which have such a need for being able to communicate with each other.

Some of the members of this commission were unfamiliar to the method of M. Sudre, so it was necessary to do some more demonstrations in their presence.

For this purpose we met at the Champ-de-Mars with the clarions which had been used before and performed once again the principal experiments described in the report of February 28; they had the same success.

Meanwhile the commission was preoccupied with the difference which exists between theory and practice, especially in the case of M. Sudre's invention. On a small scale both could obtain equal success, but on a large scale — would it be the same?

So the commission wonders if all the circumstances which might apply to this theory have been studied or exactly understood.

Finally, the commission doubts that this method is so simple that it could be taught to anyone, especially to people with limited abilities. The demonstrations regarding that specific point were not sufficiently conclusive.

The commission thinks these questions must be perfectly resolved before the country has to absorb the cost of imposing these new studies on the army.

It would also make possible for one to appreciate the merit of the recompense [for what it would pay back in benefits to the country].

Surely the best way to move toward this solution is to ask Mr. Sudre to teach the system to the commission itself, with all of its secrets, and he expressly agreed. Nevertheless, M. Maréchal, the commission wants to know what are the possibilities for a recompense, and what amount it would be possible for you to consider.

Here it is necessary to give to M. Sudre all the justice that he merits; all of his responses were with a delicate sentiment and disinterestedness.

Therefore, without any more obstacles, M. Sudre explained in a few words all the mechanisms of his method; it is so simple and so easy to understand that, after the first explanation, one of the members of the commission was able to transmit the orders contained in a vocabulary which had been communicated to him.

He did it several times, and always exactly.

After these demonstrations, M. Sudre added some comments on the further developments which his invention is capable of.

He made us understand how easy it is for the system to adapt to any circumstance, as well as those improvised by the commandant.

How can we be sure an order has been heard and understood?

How can we, by a simple transposition, send a secret message?

Finally, if all parts of the army, the battalion, squadron, and batterie are spread all over the battle field, how would it be possible to organize a vast *Téléphonie* communication, so that, at any time and at any place, the words of the chief who is in command will be heard?

At this point, the commission had only to occupy itself with the four questions which were a consequence of the favorable report of February 28, conclusions which each member of the commission was ready to approve, applying the full power of their convictions.

Here, Monsieur le Maréchal, are the questions as you posed them:

Question 1
'Examine the best way to proceed to create the necessary education which would make possible the general use of this method in all parts of the army: infantry, cavalry, artillery, and engineers.'

The commission recognizes that the method of M. Sudre is of a level of intelligence which is simple and easy. It believes it is not necessary to establish a permanent school, because within three months a teacher could be trained. It will therefore be very easy to teach in a very short time a large number of infantry clarions chosen from the garrisons of Paris and its neighborhood.

Every day the director of that school will teach the group that he will have with him in the area most appropriate, as in any other kind of exercise.

These instructions could be extended immediately to all the corps of horse and engineers, as was desired by several officers.

And the trumpet, with such a high pitched sound, because of its difficulty in playing and the restricted power of its sound, should be replaced by another instrument.

The members of the commission who belong to these armies thought it would be appropriate to take this occasion to carry out this modification and think that the clarion would be the perfect instrument to replace the trumpet with the greatest advantage.

The engineers instead of having two tambours per company, will have no trouble changing to one tambour and one clarion.

In any case, with all the resources which are available in the two divisions in Paris, it will be easy within two years to have more teachers than are necessary for all the corps of the army.

Mr. Sudre would be the preferred person to direct this school.

Question 2
'In any case, if there is to be a School of Téléphonie created, indicate the personnel which it should include: the number of teachers and the number of students from each part of the army.'

It is true that it is not enough to create teachers; it will be necessary at the same time that officers must have a practical understanding of this method, the mechanism of the sound, so they can understand all its applications and follow its progress; and finally the power to undertake and augment the necessary instruction of all the clarions of all the regiments.

The Staff School seems the perfect one to be the center for this instruction.

The students who come to this school will then take this instruction out into all of the army, during the normal training periods that they have to do, and they might even create small schools which could preserve their traditions and their methods.

In the field, these same officers, spread out everywhere, will make all of these applications sure and easy.

The commission recognizes that, in any case, these studies will not necessitate a permanent establishment; the commission thinks that two years will be sufficient both to initiate all the officers of the Staff School to the secrets of M. Sudre and all of the students in two successive terms.

The instruction will continue and perpetuate itself therefore very easily.

Question 3
'Evaluate the expenses necessary to this teaching'

The commission has shown that the application of the method of M. Sudre will necessitate no new expenses; and how this teaching will not affect the habits and service of the various corps, who perhaps will be called upon to send teachers to the rest of the army.

The only expenses will be in the form of the initial payment to M. Sudre, purchasing materials of little cost and the distribution of some small gratifications.

The annual expense will not exceed 6,000 francs.

Question 4
'Finally, what is the opinion of the commission regarding the recompense due M. Sudre for the merit of his invention and for the relinquishment of it he will make the government?'

The commission made sure that M. Sudre will not have impossible expectations. In any case, before rendering an opinion, the commission wanted to understand the smallest details of his work.

The commission recognizes that in order to give his invention all the merit and perfection that it has today, he has had to spend about 32,000 francs, and we are not talking about 20 years of personal work, exclusive and uninterrupted, which for M. Sudre represents a considerable sum of money, which one could calculate by what he would have made if he had had a lucrative job, such as the director of a music school.

The commission can not go that far. It thought that for the two years that M. Sudre will consecrate to the foundation of a *Téléphonie School* and the instruction of its teachers, it would be possible to give him an annual salary of 3,000 francs. The commission thinks that in exchange for what he will contribute to the government in giving the secrets of all his works, he should receive the sum of 50,000 francs under the title of National Recompense.

These propositions are not what M. Sudre had hoped for after such long and difficult work, but he did accept them with understanding.

The commission has already recognized the patriotism and disinterestedness that he manifests in this regard.

Also, M. le Maréchal, it is the unanimous intent of the commission that this be the minimum payment, which should in no case be reduced, and that after the two years of his teaching you can help him in making new applications which might be foreign to the needs of the army but which might be useful to other administrations, etc.

In summary, Monsieur le Maréchal, the commission believes that it is the opportune time to introduce the *Téléphonie* method of communication into all components of the army; and that everything mentioned in this report is possible without changing any traditions or without great expense.

However, the commission thinks that the technical vocabulary developed by M. Sudre can be considered only as examples and that each part of the army would have to develop its own special vocabulary, containing the phrases which are needed and specific to them.

Therefore it will be necessary to create a commission in which all the elements are represented, in order to coordinate all the vocabularies.

The method of M. Sudre is open enough that we can include all phrases specially needed by future wars.

Finally, M. le Maréchal, the commission thinks that considering all the accidents of terrain, the manner of war that we are using, Africa will open a valuable field of application to try the method of M. Sudre and use it with great advantage.

Paris, June 1, 1843
Generals Schneider
baron Duchant
baron Marbot
marquis de Lawoestine
Marérchal Bellonnet
Squadron Chief, Vaudrimey.

As the reader has seen, there was a constant progression of favorable, and even enthusiastic, reports by the military commissions, but nothing ever seemed to develop from them. By 1844, Sudre seems to have temporarily given up hope and in this year published his little history of the *Téléphonie*.

He attributed the inaction of the government to something about his *Téléphonie* which was 'so new, so vague, so magic that somehow many people are still uncertain of the possibilities of the execution of sound.' Happily, he says, the number of unbelievers diminishes each time they witness one of his demonstrations. He seemed to accept his fate with a certain resignation.

> It was the same for the movement of the earth, the discovery of steam and the discovery of the new world! The great inventors, whose names I invoke without pretending to belong to them, struggle long against the incredulous public, and pass through the most cruel trials before their genius imposes silence on their detractors.
>
> Without doubt, FOUR SOUNDS, with which one can say everything, express everything and communicate to a distance, diminish considerably all the symbols which traditionally represent our ideas. Therefore many people do not welcome this system and have a sentiment of distrust because it is based on only four notes, written or performed, yet it is a system which is as rich and varied in expression as the most extended language.
>
> What can one conclude? Nothing can resist against a man when he has persistence added to his will.

Before concluding his history of the *Téléphonie*, Sudre makes one last argument on its behalf. He lists the traditional means of signals used by the navy: signal fires, Bengal light [fireworks], bells, tambour, and cannon. With all of these, Sudre says, one can only transmit a total of 120 phrases when under sail and 40 phrases at anchor. On the other hand, the *Téléphonie* can transmit all the orders contained in the *Tactique navale*, which amount to nearly one thousand eight hundred. And in addition to that, one can make up his own orders and transmit them as the situation demands.

Sudre mentions that some of the reports thought an instrument with a stronger sound would be needed to make the *Téléphonie* feasible for military use and he indicated that he is at this moment, in 1844, working on such an instrument. In fact, Sudre mentions that on 17 April 1842, he gave another demonstration before naval officers in the Hertz Hall, in Paris, using an instrument with an air compressor which had just been invented by a M. Guérin. Admiral Mackau, the present Minister of the Navy, complimented him on both his instrument and his method.

After this Sudre apparently gave one more demonstration, in Metz, ordered by the Minister of War. He concludes his book with the hope that the Staff officers,

> will find that the *Téléphonie* will justify the good opinion of the men of art, science and war, who, after careful examination, have judged it of use to the nation.
>
> Paris, June 10, 1844　　　　　François Sudre

After 1844 we hear no more from Sudre regarding the *Téléphonie*. However we know he continued in his efforts to convince the military for another five years at least, through an article by Hector Berlioz, which appeared in the *Journal des Dèbats* for 17 November 1849. This article suggests that Sudre had once more simplified his method, now offering it in a version for only *three* pitches. Also, it appears that the officers were still worried about the sound being loud enough, so Sudre makes the startling offer to demonstrate his method by using [tuned] cannons. Berlioz describes the subsequent success of this demonstration. From Berlioz we also learn that the Minister of War had never paid Sudre the money which a commission recommended and Berlioz pleas once again for the financial recognition Sudre deserved.

As did Sudre, Berlioz also makes observations on the sad fate of inventors in general. In this regard, it is quite extraordinary to read of Berlioz's quite accurate predictions regarding the inevitable invention of the airplane!

Here, then, is the newspaper article by Berlioz.

LA TÉLÉPHONIE

> M. Sudre is offering to us at this moment a new and sad example of the fate of all the inventors in our inattentive, forgetful, and jealous society. For twenty years he has been fighting, swimming against the current, speaking, writing, demonstrating, proving that a discovery of the highest importance for armed forces of the earth and sea, and even also for the rapid propagation of pacific ideas, is in his possession. He is demonstrating that this discovery is his, that he alone made it, that he then perfected and simplified it to the point of making its use extremely easy, and for twenty years they have sent him about his business, they scorn him in a thousand ways, they make him promises not kept, in his regard they commit unspeakable abuses of confidence, and meanwhile, the poor man is using, in order to exist, his last resources and those of his friends. *La téléphonie*, or acoustical wireless, is the art of transmitting afar orders and news by means of a very small number of sounds combined in diverse manners. M. Sudre had at first employed for his sound signals the five principal notes of the clarion (*do–sol–do–mi–sol*); now his is limiting himself to three sounds (*sol–do–sol*). With these three notes he can communicate 3,159 orders. Naval tactics can only give 1,815 (in clear weather), with the aid of 34 colors, flags, or pennants. Two minutes suffice [with this new clarion system] to send three orders

nearly 2,000 fathoms, approximately. These sound signals consequently can be transmitted at night as well as during the day, in a calm atmosphere, or in the middle of mist and rain. The use of the *téléphonie* costs nothing, since in the smallest army corps there are men whose duty consists of playing the clarion.

In very little time the *téléphonie* method can be taught in a sure manner to the monitors charged with the transmission of orders and of the interpreting of those which are transmitted to them; the inventor proved it many times. To the objection that they raised of the inability of the clarion to carry sound signals to great distances, M. Sudre answered with the following proposition: 'Give me eight cannons, and by their tones, I shall say what you would like to dictate to me, to a monitor possessing the secret of my method, and placed at the extreme limit of the distance where the noise of a size 12 ordinance gun can reach.' The experiment attempted in the presence of M. the Duke of Montpensier and several superior officers, and M. Sudre being assured that the eight artillerymen that were placed at this dispositions could fire at precise moments when he so commanded, he transmitted with a very great rapidity and a scrupulous fidelity, at an enormous distance the five following orders, improvised by M. the Duke of Montpensier:

Rally the sharp-shooters!
The enemy is abandoning his position!
How much time can you stay in the position where you are?
Send us a company of light infantrymen!
Come to headquarters!

The prince and all those in attendance were struck by such a conclusive proof, and warmly congratulated M. Sudre on the excellence and the obvious utility of his ingenious invention.

All the commissions and under-commissions, named thirty different times to assure that the proof was exact and the exactitude proved, having always obtained the same result, the Minister of War, the Minister of the Navy, the Academy of Beaux-Arts, a considerable number of officers and artists were obliged to agree that the solution to the problem was complete, the utility of that method evident, and its use as sure as it was easy.

After having used on his works both the small fortune that he possessed and twenty years of his life, M. Sudre, who moreover has always refused to communicate his secret to foreign powers, who would have paid him very well for it. M. Sudre, I say, has an evident right to an honorable recompense. One commission, named by a Minister of War finally concluded, several years ago, in an *eighth report* on the *téléphonie* method, that in exchange for the ceding of the inventor's secret to the government, a sum of *50,000 francs* be allotted to him as a national recompense. This offer being accepted without observations by M. Sudre, he, believing the affair ended, communicated without reservation the key of his method to the members of the commission. And yet the *téléphonie* method has not yet been adopted officially, and the fifty thousand francs have not been given over, and the poor inventor, in order to live, is driven to the last expediencies. If he is not indeed driven mad, he will die of hunger, and it is a true scandal whose causes the Assembly of the Representatives will shortly be called upon to examine.

But this is the fatal law to which the unfortunate, bent under the weight of a new idea, have, in all times and in all places, been subjected. Two years have not passed when they wrote before, here, very seriously to prove the impossibility of the use of the electric telegraph and the absurdity of the attempts made for its application. Yet, today human thought circulates lightening fast from one end of Europe to the other, and in the northern half of America, by means of this simple wire, so ridiculed, whose conduction power [they said] would be paralyzed by the simple contact with a magpie. Napoleon did not recognize the future of steam, and Fulton, in his eyes, was only a fool, whose claims and experiments obsessed him.

> Shortly, we will have the repetition of the same spectacle for a discovery even more important, that of the directing of lighter-than-air craft by means of a combination of propellers and inclined planes. Obviously, the latter, once demonstrated and put into usage, the relations of the diverse peoples who make up the large human family will be entirely changed; an immense revolution will be accomplished whose fortunate consequences are incalculable. This is precisely why the audacious mechanic who wishes to give man wings capable of defying the winds and swooping over the storm, will experience a stronger and more obstinate resistance. He will be ruined, he will die in harness; he expects to, he is prepared for it. But navigation of the aerial ocean will nonetheless be opened to us sooner or later, and our descendants will be astonished then, because a corner of the veil had already been lifted, that their fathers, doubting for centuries the solution to the problem, should have been so seemingly determined to prowl the terrestrial crust like the most infirm animals.
>
> Time is a great teacher, true, but man is a very stupid scholar.

After the death of Sudre, the military once again expressed an interest in the *Téléphonie* and on 1 August 1864, the Minister of the Navy invited Sudre's wife to go to Cherbourg to demonstrate the *Téléphonie* at sea.

These experiments took place at night, during a torrential rain, and in spite of this all the orders given were accurately communicated. She apparently presented not only the old system, but also a new version with the numerous perfections made before Sudre died. This new version permitted the *Téléphonie* method to dictate all the naval signals by using only *three* notes [*sol, do, sol*], alternatively represented by three numbers [1, 2 and 3], by three sounds or by three 'signal-disks' during the day, or by three lanterns or three rockets during the night, one white, one blue and one red. During fog, the method could communicate by three whistles, three strikes on a tambour, by cannon, or by bells. Thus one could transmit all the orders of the day, by night or in fog. The commission, charged with judging this system, prepared another report, which was sent, together with a letter, to Mme Sudre by the admiral de La Roncière Le Noury.

> Madame,
>
> I have the honor to send to you what you asked me to give you, the report of the commission regarding the demonstration of the Téléphonie at Cherbourg.
>
> I can only associate myself with the favorable opinions given by the commission.
>
> With the homage of my respect,
>
> Admiral de La Roncière Le Noury
>
> Extract of the Conclusions of the Report of this Commission
>
> We recognize how extremely clever the principles, the combinations and the entire ensemble of the system *téléphonie* is.
>
> In our opinion the means of communication for use by the navy is, for the moment, incomplete, and could be improved in the future, inspired by the principles adopted by Mme Sudre.
>
> The system of night signals, with the lanterns particularly attracted our attention to the experiments. In this system, the geometric figures, traced by the lanterns, joined together with the differences in their size and their colors, sufficed for communicating a specific order.
>
> The system of signals during the night seems to merit serious attention.

The complete and satisfying results, obtained by the signals at night, done with the mixing of colors, we believe would be of practical advantage if adopted by the navy.

Our book of signals does not need any modification and Mme Sudre has offered to give us a *téléphonique* key which would permit us to interpret our orders.

It would suffice then to arm our ships with a certain number of colored lights in order to have at our disposition a way to transmit the orders which are most often on our minds today.

Mme Sudre has proposed to apply equally the *Téléphonie* to long distance signals, to aid the three signs adopted in the method, something which seems to us as very possible.

On obtaining the number of combinations, also considerable, this system could be the most practical.

On board the *Magenta*, Sept 19, 1864, signed Eugene Sellier and B. de Villemereuil

On returning to Paris, Mme Sudre obtained an audience with the Navy Minister, M. de Chasseloup-Laubat, before whom she also demonstrated the *téléphonie* system. He expressed his complete satisfaction and surprise at the speed of the transmission and the extreme simplicity needed to obtain such good results.

The Universal Musical Language

In about 1829, Sudre was working at revising his Musical Language, which used seven pitch symbols to represent the French alphabet, into a new system using only four pitches for the military clarion. While his earlier Musical Language was only a translation of French into music, he must have realized that in developing the new system for the military, the *Téléphonie*, he was doing something quite different. He was now using a small group of notes as a *symbol* for French words and phrases. It must have also occurred to him at that time that by extending this beyond the score of the military, to the entire French language, he would be making the first step towards the development of an universal language. He wrote of this period,

> While I was still working on the application of my method, either for the use of the army or for the navy, a philanthropic idea dominated my thoughts.
> It was an idea of generalizing this method of communication and using it for all the people of Europe. An immense project, to be honest, but the consequences would have great result: the idea that everyone would be able to understand idioms with the same sounds and bring the multiplicity of languages under the unity of the *musical language*.

The idea of a common, universal language had been the subject of French philosophers for a long time. It is apparent that, at some point, Sudre had made some study of this subject, for when he published his history of the *Téléphonie*, in 1844, he inserted, as footnotes, several quotations on this subject which were clearly of inspiration to him. We quote them here, in the order which he did, even though chronologically they are out of order.

> A unique alphabet, using all languages could bring human minds to a universal method: by simplifying the symbols, one will get the languages closer; by getting the languages closer, one will get the people closer; from the separation of people came barbarism, by getting them closer, civilization will grow.
>
> Chénier, de Academie française.

...

> What is left to be done in general in languages, is to try at least once a conventional language proposed for so long; purely real language, all consecrated to facts, the family of facts, the most common needs, the exchange and friendly transaction that are most often being needed; limited language, but sufficient, that will offer without effort, in its small sphere, all the physical relations between man and man; the universality of that language should not be more inaccessible to thought than the one of numbers; the cosmopolitan language which will only take a few days of study for civilized people and will open to all travelers of all countries; artificial language, but social, which will have the result of getting us closer together, by friendly relations, as the one of natural brotherhood.
> I am not sure that God allowed it, but it is not forbidden for the human brain to try it, and this work will be as easy in its execution as it is noble in its object. The sole experience, and it is worth it to try, can give us an idea of the possibility of its application.
>
> Charles Nodier, de Academie française

...

> Someone that could articulate a special symbol and could easily organize those characters in their philosophical order, will be very close to an universal alphabet.
> The large number of superfluous symbols shows a language in decay.
>
> Charles Nodier, de Academie française

...

> If someone had well explained the simple ideas that are in the imagination of the human being, which are composed of all that he thinks, I would hope that next the universal language would be very easy to learn, to pronounce and to write, and what is the most important, will help the judgment by explaining so distinctly all things, that it will be almost impossible to make a mistake, and I believe the science is possible.
> D'Algarno, who preceded Wilkins and Leibnitz, said that with five physical senses, five vowels and five consonants, the intellectual sense could furnish the words to all perceptions of man.
>
> Descartes

...

> Languages, idioms and dialects differ so much that often one can not understand the peasant of one's own village, while music is one for all earth.
>
> Chabanon

...

> As music is the most simple way to express one's ideas, it is for this reason that human beings at the beginning of creation, and everywhere on the globe must have, before the creation of letters, used sounds as the unique way that they had to manifest to express their emotions, and that is why music became the primitive language and consequently the universal language of the people of the globe. All earth had only lip, one way of talking (Gen. 10, v, 1–2).
> This sentence of the bible confirms our opinion, and is remarkable, because Moses used and preferred the word *labii* (for lips) instead of *lingua*, as for us to learn that then the sounds were the only way that humans could express themselves, since they needed then only the movement of their lips to make a sound and to produce more or less low sounds, more or less high sounds, and there were then no languages as we know them now, where the tongue is used to speak and there were no different pronunciations that we can distinguish today and call nasal, guttural, etc.
>
> De Vismes (from *La Pasilogie*)

...

> The first languages were singing and passionate: all the notes of music were as so many accents. In the first times, we spoke as well with the sounds and rhythm than with the articulations and the voice. Speaking and singing were once the same thing, says Strabo.
>
> J.-J. Rousseau (*On the Origin of Languages*)

Regarding this last quotation, Sudre apparently found here the genesis of his idea to make music again the international language.

> If, as Strabo says, that *speaking and singing were formerly the same thing*, there is no doubt that one gives preference to the vocal accent over the oral accent. In effect, we can see that the vocal sounds of all people of the earth can be fixed and adapted to our chromatic scale and still produce the same results. As the vocal sound of the Indian, Chinese or Laplander can be assimilated with that of the European and these sounds could be represented by universal characters, known, or easy to learn, we can conclude that ideas generally can be expressed the same way.

In the Introduction to his discussion of the application of syntax to his Universal Musical Language, Sudre elaborates on the goal of his work. First he points out that, in 1832, he found 3,064 spoken languages on earth, including 587 in Europe, 937 in Asia, 276 in Africa, and 1,264 in America! It is not surprising, therefore, he says, that philosophers have often wished for an universal language.

> Occupied for 45 years with this important question, I have always thought that the problem could not be resolved without the aid of musical notes, considering, or seeing the universality of the symbol, its uniform figures, the facility to write, pronounce and indicate by the hands, and to be appreciated by touch, made by quintuple means (five fingers) the communication of a language the most properly called universal.
>
> By the word *universal* I understood not that it would be destined to replace some of the existing languages, that was never my thought. We learn always the different idioms in order to know the scientific works, the poetry and literature of different peoples …
>
> Some hundreds of persons learn one or two foreign languages, and 20 or 30 million know nothing but their native language, and so these are the millions of individuals that I had in mind when I attempted to create a language which could unite them.
>
> It would serve, then, the common man in general, like Latin of the Middle Ages, with this difference, that instead of the necessity of three or four years of study, three or four months would suffice.
>
> Nature accords all men an intelligence sufficient in all circumstances to come to comprehend similar sounds, sometimes with the help of gesture, a most important reason if we give an easy means to express by the definite signs he will need all his life.
>
> I have therefore included all these ideas in the seven notes of music. I have expressed them in easy combinations to remember, and I have formed a language accessible to all intelligences and all the people of the world.

The first product of Sudre's efforts in developing his Universal Musical Language was apparently the assembling of a series of *Idéographique Dictionnaires*. These begin with single and two-note combinations of basic and useful words, such as 'No' (*do*), 'Yes' (*si*), 'I' (*do, re*) and 'You' (*do, me*). Next comes a dictionary of three-note combinations, again for common and useful words. These include, 'Time' (*do, re, do*), 'Day' (*do, re, mi*), 'Week' (*do, re, fa*), 'Month' (*do, re, sol*), and 'Year' (*do, re, la*).

One can already see here the impossible notion that any one could ever learn to hear the slight variations which result in nearly 13,000 different words. For example, *sol, re, sol* means 'Language,' but the change of one sound, to *sol, re,* **la**, means 'Dictionary.' In addition, in Sudre's Universal Musical Language, the entire class of a word is represented by the same symbol. Thus *sol, re, sol*, means not only 'language,' but also 'idiom, dialect, linguistics and philology!'

Now Sudre goes to four-note combinations, in what he calls seven keys [*clefs*]. Each of these separate, small dictionaries begin on the key-note indicated, although he does not show the altered notes of these keys, that is to say, in the 'Key of Re,' he continues to show *fa* and not the sharped *fa*. These seven 'keys' are used to organize his vocabulary as follows:

The Key of C includes words for 'the part of the physical and moral man, and his intellectual facilities, his qualities and his needs.'

    For example: *do, mi, sol, me* is 'Grandeur,'
                       do, mi, sol, fa is 'Intelligence.'

The Key of Re 'is concerned with objects of the toilette, that which is included in a house, to his work and the household of his family.'

    For example: *re, si, do, sol* is 'Family,'
                       re, si, do, la is either 'Grandparent.'

The Key of Mi 'is for the actions of man and his defaults.'

    For example: *me, la, fa, do* is 'Insensible,'
                       me, la, fa, re is 'Indifferent.'

The Key of Fa 'is for the country, voyages, war and the navy.'

    For example: *fa, do, re, do* is 'Nature,'
                       fa, do, re, me is 'the Country side.'

The Key of Sol 'is for fine arts and science.'

    For example: *sol, re, do, me* is 'Flute,'
                       sol, re, do, fa is 'Oboe,'
                       sol, re, do, sol is 'Saxophone,'
                       sol, re, do, la is 'Trumpet.'

The Key of La 'is for industry and commerce.'

    For example: *la, fa, la, do* is 'Measure,'
                       la, fa, la, re is 'Proportion.'

The Key of Si 'is for the village, government and administration.'

    For example: *si, re, si, do* is 'Diplomacy,'
                       si, re, si, re is 'Politics.'

Now Sudre presents a second series of dictionaries in the same seven keys, in which the four-note combinations are distinguished from the first series only in the fact that they all begin with a repeated note. In terms of vocabulary,

    The Key of Do is 'consecrated to religion.'
    The Key of Re is 'dedicated to construction and the different trades.'
    The Key of Mi is 'for propositions, adverbial locations and isolated adverbs.'
    The Key of Fa and Sol 'are for different illnesses.'
    The Key of La is 'for industry and commerce.'
    The Key of Si is 'for Justice, Magistrates and Tribunals.'

Finally, a third series of idiographic dictionaries is reserved for the 'three kingdoms of nature, the animal, plant, and mineral.' Sudre then made an alphabetical dictionary of these three series of idiographic dictionaries, and it exceeds 12,000 words!

In addition, Sudre prepared extensive and complicated rules of syntax, in which distinctions of case or gender, etc., are often indicated by a dot or line over a note, which is interpreted as an accent [*rinfortzando*] in performance.

At some point it occurred to Sudre that while he gives for 'Lion' *do, re, mi, do, re*, this musical language would have no meaning for a German unless he first knew that *do, re, mi, do, re* meant, *for him*, 'der Löwe'. In other words, Sudre came to realize that he must first translate these 13,000 words and their symbols into every language on earth, before his Universal Musical Language could become a practical reality. If, as the alternative, everyone was required to *first* know French, then French becomes the universal language and the musical language is no longer necessary.

Thus, facing an impossible task in his lifetime, he set the goal for himself of making an additional eleven dictionaries, translating his Universal Musical Language from French into German, English, Portuguese, Italian, Spanish, Dutch, Russian, Turkish, Arabic, Persian, and Chinese! According to his wife, 'he was obliged to stop for the considerable fatigue of this work profoundly altered his health.' Nevertheless, it appears that he had completed eight of these dictionaries by the time of his death in 1862.

We first hear of his progress on his work on the dictionaries in a newspaper article of 23 July 1833, in the *Le Messager des Chambres* in Paris. It is evident that by this date he had progressed to a point where he had the confidence to begin public demonstrations of the new Universal Musical Language.

> M. Sudre, inventor of the Musical Language, which has a useful application to the art of war, and also to the art of the navy, as one has noticed by the reports done for the ministers of these two departments, has now concentrated the development to his ingenious invention for application to all languages in general.
>
> After three years of research, work and perseverance, this scholarly and able musician was able to, as we say, resolve all the problems which all the philosophers before had vainly attempted until today — that of creating a universal language by means of the symbols of music.
>
> He performed yesterday a demonstration at the Royal Academy of Fine Arts and everything was perfectly successful.
>
> Several members of other academies, among whom were MM Delaborde, Tissot, Raoul-Rochette, etc., attended this interesting performance and begged M. Sudre to transmit to his student, that we had placed in a different room, words taken out of dictionaries of languages which were made as a part of his immense work, and everything was translated perfectly into French. It was the same with various phrases, which, translated musically by M. Sudre, were in the same instant translated by his student into diverse languages and always with the same success.
>
> The Academy, which has listened with particular attention to the explanations of M. Sudre of his discovery and its application, showed infinite satisfaction in its results, and also named a commission composed of members of the different academies which compose the Institut, aimed at examining all the details of the system which has already brought great honor to him who created it, and which interests at the same time the entire civilization of Europe.

The following year Sudre apparently asked to give a private demonstration for the editor of the Parisian newspaper, *La Quotidienne*. The article which followed, 'De La Langue Musicale,' published 24 June 1834, includes some interesting personal descriptions of Sudre. We also find here that he was now prepared to demonstrate his system in six languages besides French. Here is the portion of this article which relates to the Universal Musical Language.

I was thinking of other things, when someone spoke to me for the first time of the invention of M. Sudre. I had never envisioned an essay of this genre, but that is sort of a joke; of theater and of novels, I have seen lovers correspond despite teachers or jealous ones, sometimes in the air of romance, sometimes in the refrain of a little song. This was an affair of convention. I thought that M. Sudre was not acting differently; I believed that he expressed a thought, but never a phrase, never a word, and when someone announced to me the visit of this savant, I waited to be covered with torrents of harmony; I invited amateurs of music. The rumor spread that I was giving a concert.

M. Sudre arrived with his violin and two students, one of whom carried a clarion. My friends watched them; it was the first time one had seen the possibility of a duet between a violin and a clarion. In waiting for some late arrivals, I talked with M. Sudre, who, from the very first words, inspired a confidence, which his singular talent and intimate superiority had the power to create. With his southern accent, his look and his gestures, he expressed so energetically the profound conviction of a man who has given 20 years of his life to create a language which leaves nothing to be desired. While entire peoples, after centuries, still don't have [complete] terms and expressions, he tells me he has suffered deceptions and discouragements despite many satisfying experiences. And I understand: there is not only a coldness among men called to judge the genius of other men, but more often there is envy: a shameful and miserable sentiment which one finds in all of the highest and lowest degrees of the social scale, in all of the ranks, in all professions …

I would like first to tell you the experiences of which I have been a witness, and leave you to judge if it is not something exceptional.

We were in a room with M. Sudre. He had his students placed in another room and asked us to please write some words which he would transmit immediately and which his students would translate just as quickly.

I wrote this word: *victoire!*

And I waited, I confess it, if it were a fanfare, or at least bursting notes, that would have been the color of my thought. But I heard several sounds, absolutely insignificant musically, after which the student opened the door that separated us, and gave to us the word, *victoire!*

This first success made us want an encore. This full sentence was proposed: '*Les insurgés vont être cernés!*' M. Sudre repeated the phrase in music and his student didn't make us wait for the translation. We looked at ourselves without saying one word and our stupefaction did not surprise the savant: a secret which took 20 years to establish is not delivered in three seconds.

The musical language has this in particular, that it could express all the known idioms. M. Sudre asked us to say phrases in English, German, Spanish, Italian, Arabic and Chinese, as we wished. The most knowledgeable among us formed with the most trouble these three English words: 'Will you speak?'

And the student of M. Sudre was not long in telling us the English, which M. Sudre himself had expressed musically. I confess it is the only fifteen minutes of my life that I seriously regretted not knowing Arabic or Chinese.

In his turn, one of the students took his clarion and went with us while his comrade stayed alone in another room. This student gave several orders formulated by us which were repeated by his comrade with the greatest exactness. But until then we had not thought to propose anything other than ordinary words, so now we thought to choose something more difficult. We chose veritable abstractions, 'philosophiquement,' 'inquisition,' and the clarion repeated these words, as well as an algebra problem …

A German, who must forgive me for having forgotten his name, was the first to imagine a musical language, such was the one I expected. Everyone in the world could understand his language and learn it reasonably, but its usefulness was nil and the language and its author are at present completely forgotten.

This last reference is apparently to one, B. C. A. Weyrich, who published in 1830, in Leipzig, an artificial language method under the title, *Die Instrumentalton-Sprechkunst oder Anleitung durch instrumentaltone alle Nachrichten in die Ferne zu geben, sowoll in Frieden als in Kriege, beim Civil und Militair, auf dem Lande und Meere.*

In September 1834, Sudre traveled to Belgium for two demonstrations of his Universal Musical Language in Brussels. His reputation had evidently gone before him, for several newspapers published articles anticipating his first demonstration. The first of these, published in the *Le Franc-Juge*, for Sunday 21 September 1834, under the title, 'Langue Musicale,' reveals that Sudre had promised to employ six languages in his demonstration.

> M. Sudre, inventor of the musical language, has arrived in Brussels. We are permitted to attend these demonstrations full of lively interest and we appreciate that we can hear what has been related in reports of the journals. It is delightful to spread the happy news of the presence among us of this 'Prophet of Sound,' as we have nicknamed him.
>
> The most surprising results come from hard work. The untiring perseverance of M. Sudre, by means of various sounds, transmits over great distances words, orders and entire phrases. And do not believe that this means of communication used with an individual placed one league from you can be used only for one language, which would be already rather extraordinary. We can speak in French, Italian, Spanish, German, English and Russian. Twelve telegraph symbols, represented by the sound of the clarion, suffice to transmit all the combinations of human thought. The particularly remarkable thing about the invention of M. Sudre is that the use of sound is only necessary for distance, for this method can also permit a blind man to communicate with a deaf person …
>
> M. Sudre remains only a few days in Brussels, and it is amusing that the young person who will help him is from Belgium and was given instructions by the inventor of the music language for only a short time.

This newspaper, as well as the *L'Emancipation*, two days later, published extensive quotations from the various commissions which had studied Sudre's system in Paris.

The *L'Indépendant*, for 24 September 1834, suggests that Sudre was making this trip in part to raise money by charging for these demonstrations.

> We have announced, two days ago, the arrival in Brussels of the inventor of the Musical Language. M. Sudre has chosen this time [*époque*] to come to visit us, because he would profit from the huge gathering of musicians that he will find in town, and to give them an idea of his method. He has thought, with just reason, that it is by all the musicians by which he must first be appreciated. Finally, today, in order to spread intelligence to the public, without denying the importance of the invention, it remains incredible if the men of art are not there to put to rest all doubts.
>
> M. Sudre has proposed then to give next Thursday a public demonstration of his experiments, in which all those interested in science should not miss being there. We do not know yet ourselves the results of the method of M. Sudre, but we have read various articles in newspapers and diverse official reports named to examine it, which leaves us not the least doubt of the reality of the invention.

And finally, on 25 September, the day before the first demonstration, the *Le Lynx* also published a very enthusiastic recommendation that all interested parties attend Sudre's demonstration. It emphasized the more remarkable characteristics of his system: that it is literal, that Sudre has found a way to dramatically reduce the number of symbols ordinarily used for language and that the transcriber needs to know nothing of what he transcribes. Judging by the detail in this article, one must suppose that Sudre had given a private demonstration for members of the press before the public one.

> There are few of our readers who have been heard to speak of the musical language and of its ingenious inventor, M. Sudre, whom the French newspapers have mentioned so many times regarding his numerous and brilliant successes. We learn then with pleasure that M. Sudre, now in Brussels, is proposing to give a public demonstration which will resolve the great difficulties of his art.
>
> Few people know what is meant by a musical language: one thinks first of all of an harmonic convention, sometimes soft and energetic, low or fast, sad or happy, consisting finally of the sentiments he would want to express. The inventor, with the help of his student, makes come to pass the expression of his thought. This is very far from reality. These are actual phrases, words and syllables that M. Sudre expresses on the strings of his instrument, phrases, words and syllables written by a third party and repeated literally by his student placed in another room. Thus, with the aid of seven notes of the scale, this clever musician translates all the words of the language, and at some exact point it is impossible to confuse one word with another. This is the first subject of surprise for the spectator.
>
> After having some additional thoughts, nevertheless, one can conceive how one could arrive, with the aid of octaves and half-steps, at the formation of twenty-five different sounds, each one representing a letter of the alphabet. And how, with the aid of these letter-notes, it is possible to write and transmit some word of the language using a listener with perfect pitch. That such a method is not without difficulty, how surprised will our amateurs be when they hear the clever artist render an entire syllable, or an entire word, by a single note, in the manner in which a phrase of 60 to 80 letters demands only ten or twelve notes to be literally translated? Few among them, we are sure, will understand such mechanism: it is what we call the application of the stenography to music.
>
> But that is not all: M. Sudre, for whom this most ingenious invention seemed to be so simple, has found some way to not stop when translating his maternal language into music. He has managed to make his instrument speak in Italian, Spanish, German, English and Russian, with such brevity, that the longest words of the Northern languages are rarely rendered by more than two or three notes. Nothing is more strange or more incomprehensible than to watch the knowledgeable professor transmit an English phrase, Italian or German to his student, who knows none of these languages, transmitting them in insignificant sounds, and this student will give to you this phrase literally, without any misspellings, without the least mistake.
>
> At this point the listeners will cry, 'Impossible!' and we understand their incredulity. Happily there is an excellent means to stop it, it is to attend the demonstrations of M. Sudre which will take place tomorrow, Thursday, on rue l'Impératrice, in the old hall of the Conservatory, around noon. We are not afraid that, after this demonstration, one will accuse the clever artist of *charlatanisme* or the *Lynx* of exaggeration.

Following the first public demonstration by Sudre, this same newspaper published the following review.

> The demonstration of the *Téléphonie* of M. Sudre, had coincided with the repeat performance of the monster-concert and thus did not attract a huge audience; but each person there was convinced of the importance of this useful discovery.
>
> Many women wrote the phrases and words which were then translated in an instant by his student, M. Charles Dancla, without a single error. Here are several of these phrases:

> Invention is what brings man closest to God.
> The man most useful to society is the inventor.
> M. Sudre is the Mephistopheles of Music.
>
> M. Dancla received much applause for playing an *air varié* of his own composition on the violin, consisting of pleasing melodies and many difficulties. We encourage this young artist to continue his studies, which should place him among those artists of the most distinguished talent …
>
> The success obtained by M. Sudre has led to his engagement for a second and final demonstration, where the most distinguished persons will attend; and it will take place Sunday precisely at noon.

Another review of the first public demonstration appeared in the official government journal, *Moniteur Belge*, on Sunday 28 September. In addition to taking a broader view of the possibilities in which Sudre's invention might be used, the paper informs us that Sudre had by now completed six of his manuscript dictionaries, totaling an extraordinary 86,000 words!

> All of the inventions whose aim is to facilitate communication, to make possible the most rapid transport of thought, are veritable conquests for civilization, as long as they offer an immediate and direct usefulness. A new and good system of intellectual communication is given, leaving to time and genius to find the applications. The greatest difficulty is the invention of the system, the application comes, in a manner of speaking, all by itself. Can we appreciate yet all the extent of the invention of the Chappe brothers? If the telegraph mail, conveniently established, would replace ordinary mail, it would greatly improve the speed of communication. First of all we must perfect those we have already invented; then others would find practical uses and useful results.
>
> Here comes M. Sudre who has created a new language, a language which could express all, say all, and which with the means of knowledgeable combinations by the inventor, could translate in French, Italian, English, German and Russian. Five notes only are necessary for the composition of this language. The clarion, whose sound can be heard at great distances, is the vehicle.
>
> We have had testimony of the demonstrations of M. Sudre; here is what it consists of. Various members of the audience write a word, a phrase, an order of the military service, which M. Sudre transmits in the musical language on his violin or on the clarion, and his student, following, transcribes in French on paper. The words and phrases which had been proposed at the demonstration on Thursday are:
>
> > Hello.
> > I like this method.
> > The most useful man in society is the inventor.
> > M. Sudre is the Mephistopheles of music.
> > You are an angel and I love you with all of my soul.
> > One hears the cannon at the côte de Saint-Cloud.
>
> All of this was transmitted in the musical language immediately and without hesitation, and reported by the student who heard nothing but the sound carried by the instrument.
>
> The work of M. Sudre has made such immense results: not only is his invention a trait of genius; but, to bring it to a conclusion, to develop it to be what it is, required patience and complete devotion. M. Sudre has stenographed [represented] in the musical language some 86,000 words contained in six dictionaries, French, German, Italian, English, Spanish and Russian. His method is so simple, the it sufficed for his student, after only eight lessons, to know all the combinations of the new musical language.

> General Desprez, who had been named president of the military commission charged with the examination of the system of M. Sudre, has recognized all the advantages that we could obtain for the movements of troops in time of war, where success depends often on the maneuver. This system is susceptible to many other applications.
>
> We remind artists and amateurs that today, Sunday, at noon, the second and final demonstration will take place at the local Conservatory.

The only review we have found of the second public demonstration in Brussels was published by *Le Lynx* on 30 September 1834. The success of the first demonstration now produced in the audience a number of important leaders of music and education in Belgium. It is most interesting to read, and it is the only such instance we have found, that on this occasion Sudre concluded the performance by *singing* some of his own compositions!

> The success obtained by M. Sudre in the first demonstration justifies completely the praises which we have given in our issue of the 25th. The demonstration of yesterday has made his reputation among us, and judging at least from the always increasing gathering composed of the elite of society, the marvelous demonstrations of this ingenious artist are more and more welcome. It was a beautiful title of glory that the votes of the amateurs included M. Fétis, director of the Conservatory of Brussels; M. Daussoigne-Méhul, director of the Conservatory of Liége; M. Lesbroussart, director of Public Instruction and a number of other persons distinguished for their knowledge and talents, whom we cannot list ...
>
> That which brings overall merit to the invention of M. Sudre, that which makes his system of abbreviation completely incomprehensible to the most clever stenographer, is this facility by which he renders several words by one sound: [a phrase] which consists of five words [in French] was transmitted by only three sounds, while it is necessary to render stenographically the same phrase with five symbols and even more. The difference then is to the advantage of the system of M. Sudre.
>
> But that is not all: if M. Sudre limits himself to rendering the sense of the orders he is charged to transmit, without using the precise words, our astonishment would cease, for it is not impossible to bring together a certain quantity of orders purely strategically and to apply to the symbols or the notes more of less numbers. But it is not like that: it is literally that the phrases rendered are translated, and voilà, we admit it, it is impossible to conceive.
>
> The preoccupation which had so naturally followed this demonstration of M. Sudre, did not fail to bring all the attention to young Dancla. All the interest of society which was there, when he came to play some of his pleasing [compositions]. It is the highest praise we can offer this talented and remarkable young man, to say he promises France an artist of the first order.
>
> M. Sudre finished the demonstration by singing with so much taste several Romances of his own composition, among which one we especially distinguished in which the merit of the poetry rivaled the music, and certainly it is not without reason that we said at the beginning of this article that his reputation is already made among us.

Upon his return to Paris, the newspaper, *Le National*, announced on 24 January 1835, that Sudre had been invited to give a public demonstration of his Universal Musical Language at the Conservatory of Music.

> M. Sudre will give, on January 25, in the hall of the Conservatoire, a demonstration of the Musical Language and its different applications … One imagines that this savant professor will newly arrive [with the possibility] of articulating the musical language in a manner as not to leave any doubt over the possibility to establish a universal language by which one will pronounce the names of the notes instead of singing them.

This was evidently an important gathering, as the demonstration was reviewed by a number of newspapers. The first review, published under the title 'Télégraphe Musical,' on 27 January 1835, in the *Vert-Vert*, was a humorous one, focusing on the broad public uses of such a system of communication in the future. It is also interesting to see Sudre was paired with that other young radical in Paris, Hector Berlioz.

> Music marches forward without stopping; it is a new language which all the world should know, that M. Berlioz professes and M. Sudre demonstrates.
>
> In ten years all the children who are twenty years old, who will be thirty by then, would know the ABC's of Mr. Sudre and will have made their *humanities* with M. Berlioz; a dilettante forty years old will order his dinner in *mi bémol* and will talk to his lover with the *sound of a trumpet*.
>
> M. Berlioz, as everyone knows, as Arnal has proven in the last balls of the Opera, does his business at the stock market with a violin under his arm. A stock broker comes to play the highs and lows with an orchestra in his pocket and a speculator asks for 3% on *au Clair de la lune* and five with the *grose caisse*. That is to say, the temple of the Bourse will make much more noise than work. Despite what will be said, for hiding their game, Rossini and Bellini, the greatest speculators of the world, surely very well imagined that we would have two stock exchanges instead of one, the Opera and the Théâtre Italien. Lablance, Tambourini, Rubini, Mlle. Grisi and Mme. Damoreau are speculators who handle marvelously their affairs as well as their [bank] notes. One will play overtures as one plays at the rent, and the fugue will replace bankruptcy.
>
> But before becoming a master it is necessary to have been a student, and M. Sudre is in charge of our musical and financial education: he teaches solfége and bookkeeping. We doubt any supreme method, like all reasonable men doubt miracles; but doubt is no longer permissible.
>
> For the second time, day before yesterday, we have seen and heard M. Sudre, in the hall of the Conservatoire, and there is no reason to doubt that within a year M. Panseron could ruin Rothschild.
>
> We have seen the telegraph of M. Sudre function, and we predict the ruin of all of the present telegraphs of day and night. All of the diplomatic notes will be transmitted in musical notes, which will unconsciously conduct us to an universal peace, put all people in agreement, and reestablish good harmony in the world as God made it.
>
> To sing out of tune would now become a capital sin like the lie, a crime against the nation like perjury.
>
> Myself, I believe in the wisdom of nations, I believe in the infallibility of common sense, I know well that they have a hidden meaning in each of the phrases borrowed from army vocabulary: the cannon is only a clarinet, the necessary instrument of all the overtures of peace that would be in the future. It is the tuning note which must make us in accord with Europe.

Two days later the *Le Corsaire* published a review under the title, 'Demonstration of the Musical Language.' This reviewer was particularly astonished that Sudre had been able to reduce the hundreds of sounds used in the major languages to only those of the musical scale.

> M. Sudre is the inventor of a musical language, the universality of which would be of benefit to all people, if it were possible to implant it in all the countries of the world. But how can we hope that the despotic governments will ever permit the same means of civilization and brotherhood? And, in addition, what will become of the nationalities?
>
> The system of M. Sudre is brilliant and ingenious according to all reports. First of all, he speaks indifferently of the eyes, hearing and the touch; he simplifies the symbols of thought in a prodigious manner, to the point, in the case of the *Téléphonie,* of reducing to twelve the five hundred symbols employed by the government's telegraph, and with the maritime signal he is even more admirable. Also the inventor has attained a veritable triumph in the demonstration he gave last Sunday at the *Conservatoire de musique.*
>
> M. Sudre replaces all the symbols of the living and dead languages with seven monosyllables, *do, re, mi, fa, sol, la, si,* employed without any rhythm in one or other of the twelve keys [*tons*] of music. With the aid of a violin, or any other instrument, he plays some notes, forming the translation in musical language of a phrase given by someone in the audience; and then his student, placed in another room, comes out to write on a black board the phrase he has heard on the instrument, and the remarkable thing is he never made a mistake.

The journal, *Le Ménestrel*, also reviewed this demonstration in their issue of 1 February 1835. Here we see for the first time, a fear which will be expressed by many, including Berlioz, that because of the failure of the French government to act, Sudre might be tempted to sell his system to another country. This reviewer makes the important point that in one of the possibilities of Sudre's musical language, that of simply pronouncing the names of the notes, rather than playing them on an instrument, one could use the system even if he knew nothing of music. This is also one of several newspaper reviews which suggest that Sudre should be considered an inventor on the level of Gutenberg.

> M. Sudre is one of those rare and perseverant men, who work constantly for a single goal, despite the times or the circumstances, finishing everything in triumph over every obstacle which indifference and routine throw in profusion before him. Yes, we await with confidence, while the inventor of the musical language conquers the resistance of several men, the negligence of others and the apathy of many. The notion of national glory would have to be removed from the politicians if this invention should go to foreign countries.
>
> After I don't know how many years, M. Sudre has occupied himself with the principle of his vast system: the votes of the authorities, the most honorable praise, the most sincere admiration, has come in diverse intervals, and *en masse,* to encourage the inventor, to support his projects, and to sustain his efforts.
>
> The wishes of this man would have been realized [already] if measured by the public admiration and if not for the fact that he desires to keep the honor of his work for France. The enthusiasm which the new applications have made last Sunday in the hall of the *menus-plaisirs,* could not be described. Because M. Sudre, whose brain never rests, comes to add to his *Téléphonie* system a new discovery even more prodigious yet than all the results of his first invention. The point was never lost that it was a *universal language,* by means of which one expressed all of the ideas by the simple articulation of seven notes of music. Without understanding the theory of music, any person could render his thoughts intelligible to all, by simply knowing the names of seven notes of the scale.
>
> We have seen, without understanding them, the results of this admirable discovery, and all the spectators were struck like ourselves.

M. Sudre has renewed his demonstrations of his clarion and his telegraph. Many words and phrases, written in diverse languages by the public, and applied to the *Téléphonie*, have been reproduced by his two students with remarkable fidelity.

To the number of phrases which the *Téléphonie* and the spoken language have been charged to reproduce, we have remarked the following:

> Will France force the inventor to turn to another country?
> Gutenberg has a statue in Mainz: Wait!

The sense of this last thought was understood and strongly applauded by the audience.

Four days later, *Le Pianiste*, a journal 'for piano, the lyric theater and concerts,' gave a particularly glowing account of the demonstration at the conservatory. Again, this reviewer expresses both his concern that the government might allow this idea to travel to another country and also equates Sudre with Gutenberg.

> If genius consists of conceiving a new idea, grand and useful, in seizing all of its reach, pursuing it without becoming discouraged by obstacles, developing it, pushing it finally to the highest point of perfection that it could attain, surely M. Sudre is a man of genius, and of a superior genius.
>
> All the world knows that this artist is the inventor of the musical language, a universal and precise language, and that the principles are of a simplicity and an irreproachable clarity. We regret not having before our eyes the various reports made by the Academy of Sciences and of the Fine Arts, in which are exposed the numerous advantages that we could get from this invention, but we cannot pass in silence the various demonstrations which we have attended, the 25th of last month at the Conservatory. [This demonstration] excited in all the audience a worthwhile admiration, and one much more flattering for M. Sudre in that the audience was composed principally of enlightened and distinguished men capable of appreciating it.
>
> The system of M. Sudre consists of expressing all possible thoughts, even the most abstract, by the means of seven notes of music. We can conceive easily all of the things we could get by such a process (carried, I repeat, to the highest degree of perfection), above all in the case where it is impossible to communicate by writing or by voice: particularly in the battle fields, in the valleys and mountains, from one side of a river to the other, on the sea, in the obscurities of night, that the application could be made with a complete and indisputable success.
>
> We cannot conceive [why] the government, sufficiently enlightened over the merit of this beautiful invention, does not appropriate its use. We can affirm without fear of contradiction that all men who are friends of national glory and filled with a sentiment of patriotism, would feel extreme pain that foreign countries might enrich themselves with the work of this remarkable genius, as much because of the pains, the research and studies have cost the author, as due to the admirable results it has produced and could produce in a thousand important circumstances.
>
> If it happens, and we hope not, that M. Sudre could not receive personally the advantages that he has the right to attain for his invention, and he has the pain of witnessing the indifference of his contemporaries, we would regret it sincerely, and we would not be afraid of accusing of this guilty indifference the persons who are in a position of giving recompense for such work. When it comes to posterity, that which M. Sudre already belongs to, we are assured that he will be most appreciated, and that, if we have elevated a statue of Gutenberg, the inventor of printing, we will find it just later to erect one to the inventor of the musical language.

A final review of the conservatory demonstration appeared in the *Le Philantrope Universel*, 'Journal des Améliorations sociales,' for 5 February 1835.

> M. Sudre read first of all a succinct description of his method and of the reports which had been by the various commissions. Following this he asked for members of the audience to write phrases they wanted him to transmit to his student, hidden behind a screen. With the aid of a violin, he expressed in the Musical Language the phrase that we had proposed to him, and the student right away came to write on the blackboard, to the applause of those assembled ...
>
> All of the diverse attempts were perfectly successful, and have assured the inventor of a language which could become universal, and the admiration of all the friends of science and the arts. Among other phrases proposed, one noticed this remarkable one, 'Gutenberg has a statue, Wait!' This noble and generous thought excited the enthusiasm of the audience; we hope that it will find an echo in France.

The following month, on 22 February, Sudre gave a demonstration before a cultural society known as the *Athénée*. A review in *Le Temps*, of 27 February 1835, tells us that Sudre was now also beginning to demonstrate the possible applications of his Universal Musical Language for use by the blind and deaf through a system he devised in which one hand served as the musical staff and the other pointed to where the appropriate notes would be placed.

> We already know of the invention of M. Sudre: several commissions, named from one side of the Institut to the other, and by the ministers of war and navy, have rendered for so long favorable accounts. His musical language having presented useful applications in many of the cases where the means of oral communications or telegraph would have no use. In war, at sea, in the presence of high interferences, in the obscurity of the night or in a tempest that would intercept ordinary signals, the clarion of M. Sudre has rendered valuable services. Here is something we can agree on unanimously.
>
> Unfortunately good ideas are slowly propagated: we believe we do enough by praising them, but we have left them on their own to find their way. That is what has happened to M. Sudre. His musical language is again as inactive as the theory, and despite the honorable reports of the most distinguished savants, the most competent artists, the generals of all the armies, it has again descended into a state of no useful part in practice. M. Sudre is occupied alone in the popularization of his invention.
>
> That which must reassure for his future, is that the public appreciates the merit. We have seen the proof at the demonstration he gave at the *Athénée* central in the passage du Saumon, on Sunday, February 22. He had there people of all classes, women, artists, savans, men of the world: the applause was unanimous. M. Sudre had for his assistant a student barely fifteen or sixteen years old. It was a curious thing to see the master dictate on his violin various successive notes which the student translated so rapidly on the blackboard in words of the common language. The phrase had been given extemporaneously by the spectators, and no one could be tempted to suspect in all of this any sort of trickery [*charlatanisme*].
>
> Other demonstrations have followed. M. Sudre has closed the eyes of his student, and has transmitted to him by means of only his fingers the phrases communicated by the audience; a musician of the 37th regiment is placed in an extremity of the hall and transmits on his clarion, in accents vigorous and pronounced; and several words given by a native Englishman in his own language are immediately retrieved and written on the blackboard with the corresponding telegraphic symbols. M. Sudre had explained how, in the circumstance where the telegraph lines might be interrupted by an accident, the clarion could supply with its sounds which carried a distance of 2,200 *toises*.

The final demonstration consisted of the spoken musical symbols: the master said the names of the notes and the student translated them. The same with words less common, the names of cities and of men, could not fail to be communicated by this method, which for the system's representing not the sense but the sounds there is no need to insist on these advantages.

The audience had understood, and certainly the inventor has found already a reward from his work in the flattering approbation of which he was a witness.

On 1 March 1835, *Le Ménestrel* published a review of this demonstration which was particularly enthusiastic.

> The invention of M. Sudre acquires each day more reputation in the capital. A lot of people gathered last Sunday in the grand gallery of the *Athénée*, to attend the *téléphonic* demonstrations of this tireless man. M. Sudre has obtained a most glorious success: with each of his applications, the most lively applause thundered through the hall, and the public left after this demonstration, happy to have witnessed this admirable discovery.
>
> Already the invention of the musical language is appreciated by the masses; already the rights of the inventor have been acclaimed by the organs of the press and all the scholarly authorities and artists. Only inexhaustibly bad [faith] would resist longer this universal vote of support.
>
> The *Téléphonie* and its brilliant successes are now sufficiently known to the world of literature, the musical world, the world of thought, and everything which excites in the sphere of the arts and sciences; more than once the public admiration has been manifested, to be echoed in the highest places.
>
> I wish the organs of public opinion could newly call to the attention of our government this useful discovery and the inappreciable consequences to our country.
>
> Since 1817, M. Sudre has continually occupied himself to make fruitful an idea which his passion for music had given birth, and which his love for science has driven him to develop.
>
> This idea consists in substituting all the spoken languages with a musical language whose principle is universal, and in any country on earth we could alter without destroying completely the laws of nature.
>
> M. Sudre has arrived at the goal of his efforts; he has resolved the problem of a musical language.
>
> The applications of his system can be divided into two parts: the one has a moral and philosophical goal, it could take the character of bettering human intelligence; the other presents useful and positive material for the government, from the fact of its means of communication from afar, by day, by night, over land or sea, whatever the weather.
>
> The method of application of the *Téléphonie* consists in transmitting ideas and corresponding sounds, by means of the voice or an instrument, notably the clarion.
>
> In other words, M. Sudre has found the means of introducing the method of stenography in the *Téléphonie*. Twelve symbols of the telegraph are represented by twelve sounds to be sufficient to communicate all ideas.
>
> Finally, two new applications have been recently imagined by the inventor: the first consists of making communication possible between a blind and a deaf man; the second consists of a universal language, with the aid of spoken notes of music.
>
> Various reports made by scholars, the general and superior officers, leaders of the navy and addressed to the Ministers of the Interior, War and Navy and Public Instruction, have rendered brilliant justice to the invention of M. Sudre.
>
> Among the most flattering testimonies furnished by the various commissions, one must mention the report of the Royal Institut de France, in the name of its five academies, which has recommended the system of M. Sudre in the most energetic manner, declaring that it would render service to the State and bring honor to the country.

Another review of this same demonstration, in the *Moniteur du Commerce*, of 3 March 1835, reveals that Sudre was now beginning these evenings by reading to the audience excerpts of the various reports of government commissions. This review also announces a new demonstration, to be held 15 March.

> M. Sudre has given on last Sunday, February 22, at the *Athénée* central, a demonstration of the musical language and its different applications. Before a numerous and brilliant audience, the scholarly artist had made known to the public extracts and conclusions of four reports, which had been made and addressed to the government over this valuable [*precieuse*] discovery. Following this, he began his demonstrations which consisted of dictating with the aid of a violin or another instrument, the words or phrases by members of the audience, after which the translation was immediately made by his student. He has also proven by the means of seven notes indicated by *touch*, over or between the fingers of the hand, that it was easy to establish communication between a blind man and a deaf-mute.
>
> But one application which seemed to us the most extraordinary, of which we can only render an account, is that the means of seven spoken notes can render all the combinations of thought; thus seven tones replace the four or five hundred different sounds used by different languages. It is necessary, really, to see this this prodigy of the human mind [*esprit*] to be convinced of such beautiful results ...
>
> Mr. Sudre will give, on Sunday, March 15, a final demonstration, and we encourage all the friends of letters, the arts and sciences to attend, toward convincing them, like ourselves, of the marvelous results of the *language* and the different applications which honor infinitely him who is the author.

A review in the *L'Impartial* for 5 March 1835, mentions both the Conservatory and the first *Athénée* demonstrations. It tells us that Sudre used six different languages in the latter performance and mentions both a forthcoming demonstration at the Paris City Hall and Sudre's plans to tour England.

> We are late, with regard to M. Sudre. It is not that his ingenious and useful invention has not already found in this newspaper its just encouragement, but during this time he has brought some perfections to this musical language. As he has found the means of applying so many combinations, it would be an injustice to ourselves to not add our praise to the applause he has merited in his last demonstration that he made earlier in the Conservatory of Music and in the *Athénée* central.
>
> Surely, it is the work of genius (and who can doubt it?), to conceive of a new idea, to calculate all of its importance, and not stop before finding everything it is susceptible of, and bringing it to the highest point of development. M. Sudre is a man of our times who [deserves] the highest merit of science.
>
> It is not rare, at the present time, to see the signs of public admiration for false discoveries. But invented or not, the ideas remain in the brain of he who has proclaimed to have invented them. He is content to express them, in terms more or less vague, in articles in newspapers, he hides behind the superiority of his genius, [rather than] come down from the high regions of theory, to the menial [level] of the practical. Also, the false invention, unfruitful for the country, does not gain the same appreciation of public opinion and the inventor does not enjoy a durable reputation.
>
> M. Sudre marches to a different drummer. After having gained the votes of the Royal Institut de France and of other groups of scholars, after having proven, by demonstrations made before the leaders of the army and navy, the services which the musical language, applied to an instrument in common use (*le clairon*) could render in times of war, he did not disdain from offering the fruit of his research for judgment before all men competent to judge and conceive an exact idea of it.

So it has now been proved to everyone, that the musical language could express all of our possible thoughts, even the most abstract, by means of seven notes of music. We conceive then the advantages one could get from such combinations, pushed to its highest point of perfection, one could [profit from it] above all in the case where it is impossible to communicate by written or spoken words. The Musical Language has another advantage: it is applicable to all idioms. In the demonstrations given by M. Sudre, last Sunday at the *Athénée*, the phrases which were transmitted by the clarion had been dictated by members of the audience in *six different languages*.

It has been announced that a new demonstration, next week, will take place at the Hôtel-de-Ville; the highest functionaries of the capital must attend. This performance, it is said, will be the last. M. Sudre is returning to England. Would the government allow a foreign country to enrich itself by this remarkable discovery? The minister who provides money to encourage useful inventions, should he judge this undeserving of his interest?

The important newspaper, *Le Moniteur Universel*, also reviewed the *l'Athénée* demonstration. It began its account by more or less copying the first three paragraphs of the *Le Pianiste* review of the conservatory demonstration quoted above. Then it offered some details of the *l'Athénée* evening.

First of all, having converted a phonetic language to music, he dictates with the aid of a violin, or any other instrument, the words or phrases that are proposed to him, and which his student hears and writes down in an adjoining room. In addition, he covers his eyes with a handkerchief and, by means of touch, he transmits equally all of the ideas; and, finally, he communicates them with only seven notes which he articulates in the place of performing, as one would speak in any other language.

This last application visibly surprised us, and the results will seem immense to all men who know that the diverse languages each have in particular four or five hundred different sounds, necessitated by the combinations of vowels and constants. In contrast, M. Sudre would employ but seven sounds, by which he nevertheless expresses all the combinations of thought.

His system, as we have seen, formed by the signs, characters and sounds, which are common to all civilized people, and which everywhere offer to the eye and to the mind the same resources, the same results, could perhaps one day become of general usage, since he removes all difficulty of pronunciation.

Following this, the *Moniteur Universel* quoted nearly all of the report of the Institut de France, which it had originally published in 1833.

On 12 March 1835, the *Le Philantrope Universel* announced that a second demonstration would be given at the *Athénée* three days later. In this article, entitled 'Langue Musicale Universelle,' as well as in the review following this demonstration, we can see public interest moving from the military applications of Sudre's work to a more philosophical interest in the idea of a universal language. Indeed it may well have been these two demonstrations for the *Athénée*, an intellectual and cultural society, that stimulated this change in focus. By the end of his life, Sudre was no longer referred to as an inventor, but was honored for work in philology.

For a long time the scholars have hoped to establish a universal language, a manner in which all men could transmit their ideas; but until today their efforts were in vain. The *Court de Gébelin*, in its immense effort, has given well several general etymologies by means of which we have arrived at the near certitude of an original language, which was the mother and source of all the dialects which are spoken today in the various countries; but [between] this science of etymology and the practice of a popular language, there is a large gap, and this gap can probably never be filled.

How useful one language could be to men, as a means of communicating their ideas by words, as they do by symbols and gestures! If it is impossible, or at least extremely difficult, to arrive at the formation of a parallel language, it is necessary to find then an invention of symbols or sounds which could make known their ideas. This language of symbols and sounds, like those of gestures, once accepted, could be easily adopted by all men; and it would surmount the difficulty in pronunciations and the variety of accents. It would not be stopped by differences in conception, the order and logic of the various languages or the expression of things by a symbol or a sound, thus it is impossible that those who hear would not understand.

In summary, such is the work of M. Sudre; such is the principal idea which motivates him in his researches and which has brought us the invention of the musical language, as was declared in a report made by the Royal Institut de France on February 23, 1828. After this time, useful applications have been made by this admirable method. The reports that we have seen with our own eyes have been of the most flattering praise and have completely justified the immense advantages which this system of communication has applied to the art of war, as well as in the service of the navy.

But not only has he succeeded in finding in the seven modulated notes of music in an instrument, or simply articulating the names of the notes, the means of universal communication must powerfully contribute towards bringing closer the men of the different nations. M. Sudre wanted again to make participatory the benefits of his valuable discovery to the unfortunate, in whom nature or an accident has deprived of the ability to speak, to hear or to see. So, with the seven notes indicated by touch, over or between the fingers of the hand, which represents the scale, M. Sudre can put into communication the blind and the deaf.

For the rest, in the diverse demonstrations where the inventor has shown his method, a very large public, composed of men of all classes, artists and scholars, have proven by their unanimous applause, their interest in the progress of a discovery which expands science and brings honor to the country. We also, we encourage M. Sudre to persist in his laudable efforts, to popularize his invention, and one day his name, after the example of Gutenberg, will acquire the right of recognition of all peoples.

Next Sunday, March 15, the final demonstration of the musical language will be given at one o'clock in the grand hall of the *Athénée* central, passage du Saumon.

The first review after this demonstration appeared in the *Le Réformateur* on 21 March 1835, and this writer also had a philosophical perspective.

It is a measure of manifold and perfect human knowledge, that we tend to reduce everything to its simplest elements. This law can be verified everyday, as well in the intellectual world, in physics, in chemistry, in *physiologie végétale*, in optics, also in calculus, grammar and in the social sciences: the general does not produce a satisfying agreement in application.

We have not studied enough the nature and laws of language to reduce it to its final simplicity, to generalize its admirable processes, to obtain with the least means possible the greatest results. All that we have at present tried, regarding a universal language, reduces it to groping and dreams. Following this analogy, like all ideas which have returned in different forms, in different minds, at different times, it has something of truth and of abundance. No one doubts that the very simple and well-resolved conventions which have been found in nature are the same with language, and that we could find and easy and unique means, and at the same time infinitely variable, to communicate our thoughts. It is that which M. Sudre has attempted, and which until now he alone has held the secret, but whose results have merited the encouragement of the Academy of Science and by the applause of the public. He reduces language in all its entirety to seven musical notes, which he translates by their corresponding sounds, also by the articulation of the names of these notes, every word, every idea. He applies his system to telegraphic communication, it reduces to only twelve symbols, and he transmits by the simple sounds of the clarion all the most complicated orders. He reduces, finally, the language to touch, which makes it possible that the deaf could communicate with the blind, and the demonstrations which have been given with his method seems to satisfy all the claims of the state of this new science, and we are not afraid to call it science.

Another review of the second *Athénée* demonstration appeared in the *Le Courrier Français* for 23 March 1835. Once again a newspaper wonders why the government has not taken advantage of this new discovery.

> The inventor of the Musical Language, more justly named the Universal Language, has not ceased to better his curious and useful discovery, in a variety of applications, or in multiplying the results. A public demonstration, recently given by M. Sudre, has demonstrated the numerous advantages of this new idiom, to be used nearby or at a distance. M. Sudre successively employed it as, [1] a means of the communication of thought, with the aid of a violin or any other instrument; [2] as a means of communication between a blind and a deaf man, by means of hearing and touch; and [3] as a spoken language, not necessitating any knowledge of the theory or practice of music (because the symbols could be changed at will).
>
> Finally, M. Sudre has repeated the demonstrations of the *Téléphonie*, applicable to the art of war and for the service of the navy, as has been noted, moreover, in the reports of the royal Academy of Fine Arts, the Ministers of War and Navy and in the name of the five academies of the Institut de France. We do not believe that a discovery had ever received more impressive testimonies and we refuse again to think that to gather the fruits, the inventor should be obliged to leave his country.

During the Summer of 1835, Sudre traveled to England to give a demonstration of his Universal Musical Language in London. His arrival was first announced in the *Mechanic's Magazine* in the issue of 4 July 1835.

> Mr. Sudre is now in London, where he has come to present all the details of his invention to the English public. It seems to us, in spite of the serious and important reports we have cited in its favor, he has received only feeble encouragement from his own country. We hope he will find a better fortune among us. His system, in general, is very simple and it seems to us that it is capable of producing far reaching advantages.

This demonstration occurred on 8 July 1835, in the King's Theater, and was reviewed the following day in the *Morning Herald*, in an article titled, 'The Musical Language of Mr. Sudre.'

> Mr. Sudre, whose invention has been received with great favor in France, has demonstrated yesterday, in the Concert Hall of the Theater of the King, the means, as new as it is useful, to communicate thought by means of symbols and sounds borrowed from music. The demonstration proved, first, that he had the merit of inventing a system analogous to that of stenography, by which the syllables of words could be rendered with singular rapidity. He employs, in this regard, the seven notes of the scale and the syllables of solfége. That a child has been instructed and understands the mystery of the system proves the power and precision of his method. So, a member of the audience gives him a phrase, in whatever language he wishes, written on a piece of paper. Mr. Sudre speaks it on his violin,

and the child gathers the separated words and writes [the results] with a chalk on a blackboard, while at the same time Mr. Sudre himself writes the phrase on another blackboard which only the audience can see. The results obtained yesterday, after numerous trials, prove the invariable precision of the system. It was the same when Mr. Sudre, putting down his violin, pronounced in solfége a phrase given by the audience and the child returned the translation with the equal speed. This system can also be made effective with the fingers. The great utility of this system is in its application for the army and navy, in transmitting orders from boat to boat, from one post to another, by the sound of the trumpet. For anyone who knows nothing of stenography, it is a great surprise to see Mr. Gurney include 100 lines of ordinary writing in ten or even five lines of stenographic writing. Must he not be [even more] surprised in this new system of *multum in parvo* [which produces more with less means]? In both systems arbitrary symbols express some of the ideas. In France, the military, navy and academic commissions have given Mr. Sudre the most flattering praise over the real merit of his ingenious system. This alone should suffice for recommending this to the attention of the public. The efforts required for arriving at this result have required great perseverance and a high intelligence which should not be allowed to pass without recompense.

On 10 July 1835, the *Times* of London published a review under the title, 'The Universal Musical Language.' Here is that portion of the review which discussed this topic.

Mr. Sudre, the French scholar, has given, last Wednesday, a demonstration of the Universal Musical Language, in the course of which he made several interesting experiments to demonstrate the different applications of his system, and also the possibility to put into practice this means of communication by notes of music, with the trumpet or the clarion. His demonstration was divided into two parts. In the first, he had begged those present to write on a piece of paper whatever words or phrases they wished, which he proposed to communicate to one of his students, who was placed in another end of the theater, by means of his violin. The success was equal to the promise made by the author; the student repeated verbally each written word which had been transmitted by the instrument. Mr. Sudre also exhibited an ingenious means of communication by eye, by ear and by touch with deaf and mute people.

On the same day, 10 July, a review appeared in the *Morning Post* which drew an interesting parallel to the use of communication by wind instruments in other societies. This article also mentions that this demonstration was conducted in six different languages.

The ingenious Frenchman, Mr. Sudre, has produced a means of communication of all kinds of ideas, the most complicated as well as the most simple, in a series of musical expressions. He gave, Wednesday morning, in the grand Concert Hall of the King's Theater, a demonstration of that which he has developed, in a manner most satisfying and inclusive all the applications of his ingenious system. The instrument of communication which he used for the first proof was the violin; for the second he used a *cor français*; however one can obtain the same results with any instrument. A series of phrases, gathered at random among the members of the audience, was translated by Mr. Sudre in his musical language and simultaneously communicated by another individual, his student, who was placed at a considerable distance. This individual, as soon as he received the sounds, expressed on one or other of the previously mentioned instruments, translated them in large letters with chalk on a blackboard. At other times he repeated verbally the phrases, and other times he rendered them in written musical notation (because in this system the notation is both concise and sufficient), in the language in which it had been received, or in the musical phrases which Mr. Sudre had interpreted.

That this system is applicable to all modes of enunciation known today, that it has the legitimate and incontestable right to the title 'Universal,' for that which regards the communication of ideas, we can give the greatest testimonial against any kind of doubt. We were witnesses to that which could be produced in six different languages and all with the same results. The fact that Mr. Sudre has founded his system is not new in the history of the means of enunciation employed by man, for covering distances. Those persons who have heard the cornets d'Uri [Alp horns] resonating in the valleys of the Swiss, or who have seen the effects produced in our day by the savage and civilized societies (in Central America, for example, or Ireland), by certain combinations of sounds produced by great wind instruments, these persons, we say, understand perfectly the truth of our observations. But we believe, in strict justice, according the merit of Mr. Sudre having applied to these imperfect elements the creative power of genius, and putting them into distinct forms, which, in proper perspective, promises to be as useful for humanity as were the characters invented by his predecessor, Cadmus.

This review concluded by observing that the characters are very simple and consequently very easy to learn.

The following day, the *Literary Gazette* mentioned having attended this demonstration and urged its readers to attend any following demonstrations.

> The big news today is the demonstration where Mr. Sudre has explained his Universal Musical Language, of which he is the inventor. For he who has neither seen nor heard this system put into practice, it would be necessary for us to write a long article to give a sufficient idea of it. We recommend to our readers to go and judge for themselves this invention in the coming demonstrations which will be given by Mr. Sudre …

Sudre returned to Paris for a public demonstration which was given on 20 July. A review in the *Le Voleur*, for 25 July 1835, provides us with a rare description of a composite manuscript dictionary of six languages, which we suspect no loner exists. This new manuscript was apparently submitted to the Institut and, once again, a committee recommended his work to the government. This review reads, in part,

> M. Sudre has created a polyglot dictionary, for French, Italian, Spanish, English, German and Russian. This work is intended to establish an ideographic communication of all the idioms, bring them to the common center of the musical language. A great dictionary places in the first column the musical symbols; in the following columns we see the words expressing in six languages the same idea. The author has composed, finally, for each language six individual little lexicons, where the alphabetical word is followed by the musical symbols. Each small lexicon, in turn, refers to the grand dictionary, where one finds the translation in six languages, and to which one can add without trouble translations of any other language.
>
> As for the means of the process, M. Sudre expresses and makes understood the words of all the idioms with the same sound, and brings back the multiplicity of the idioms to the unity of the musical language.
>
> Newly submitted to the Academy of Fine Arts, in his demonstration of last July 20, M. Sudre [exhibited] the dictionaries. His prompt demonstrations, repeated decisively, have excited the most lively satisfaction, and almost enthusiasm, among the scholars, who are already familiar with the marvels which have come from this inventor. He answered in English to question made in German, etc. The system was broken apart, examined in all of its facets, and submitted to all of the proofs.

> M. Sudre constantly monitored that which he had combined and has thought of everything. His system had attained perfection, and fulfilled the important conditions to be useful, applicable and easy. A commission composed of MM. Delaborde, Berton, Raoul-Rochette, Tissot, de Prony, etc., prepared a new report which, without reservations, called the attention of the government to this valuable discovery.
>
> The musical language could also be transmitted by sight, by the means of three lines, over or between which the notes are placed, the same as in ordinary music; it can be transmitted by touch, the manner favored by the blind and the deaf.
>
> The musical language or *Téléphonie* is a *savante* discovery, valuable, and with an easy and incontestable application.

Immediately after this demonstration in Paris, Sudre returned to London for another demonstration there. His host, on this occasion, was the Duke of Sussex, who was president of the Royal Society of London. In a review in the *Morning Herald* we find that Sudre was now prepared to demonstrate his system in *nine* languages, including for the first time Swedish and Dutch.

> Mr. Sudre, the inventor of the musical language, whose name has already more than once been mentioned honorably in the press, comes to be present before His Highness, the Duke of Sussex. The French savant made several demonstrations before His Highness to prove the possibility of the application of his *Téléphonie* system to all the different languages. The Duke expressed his satisfaction with the rapid and complete results of these demonstrations. He congratulated the inventor on the success of his work, as well as his perseverance, and was good enough to add that he believed it would render a service to his country, in making known a discovery which, in his opinion, would be of use to all civilized nations. Mr. Children, secretary of the Royal Society, was present at this reception, as well as chevalier Bernardi, a scholar of Romance Languages, who had written the phrases which were dictated by His Highness in Hebrew, Greek, Italian, French, Spanish, German, English, Swedish and Dutch. Despite the difficulties in inflections and aspirations of all these different languages, M. Sudre, by means of his instrument, communicated them with a precision which was all the more surprising when one considers that the young student, who had been placed at the end of the long gallery of the magnificent library of His Highness, repeated them exactly even though he did not know any of the languages. Several other scholars attended this demonstration, which lasted more than one hour, and during which His Highness had given proof of an extraordinary memory in citing several cases in which the musical language could have been employed with the greatest advantage. He examined, with an attention truly flattering for the author, the successive improvements which he had brought to his system and, on Mr. Sudre's departure His Highness told him, with the urbane manners which characterize him, that he was happy to have made the acquaintance of a man of such merit, and he would do everything in his power to give a favorable introduction in England, of a system which had such utility for both the military and the commercial world.

The next demonstration in London was again held in the King's Theater and was reported by *The Panorama of London* on 31 July 1835. This writer, identified as 'Dr. B.,' was drawn to a discussion of several interesting instances which illustrate the nature and power of communication itself.

The diversity of languages is without a doubt one of the greatest obstacles for the progress and enlightenment of civilization. It is the limits of each empire, that the language we speak poses for foreigners a barrier most difficult to surmount, as the walls of China prevented the invasions of the Tartars. The smallest thought, right now, cannot be made universal until it has been subjected to numerous transformations of the expression. How many times have we seen examples in which the thought has changed its form, in translation from one language to another, and after a while it is completely unrecognizable. One of the benefits which result from conquests, and maybe the only real one, is the bringing together numerous states under one law and one language. It is in this sense that the conquerors have accomplished a law providential to civilization.

How many centuries would it have required for the message of Christ to have spread if he had been born at a time when the Roman republic did not extend beyond the hills of Rome or the River Tiber? On the contrary, how much sense it made for the apostles to go the Rome, mistress, under the Caesars, of the civilized universe. It had only one law, one language and one ruler and that was Rome: the highest capital. Order had been brought, under the wings of the Roman eagle, to the ends of the known world, and it was in the capitol that the disciples of Christ chose to make known the rays of evangelistic light. A common language of all people, then, would be beneficial for progress in spreading civilization.

Regarding this point of view, the universal language invented by Mr. Sudre is in progress, and its application could be followed in its pleasing results, even if this language were adopted only by scholars. In effect, how much time is lost in their better discoveries, for their most useful works, after their translations have been done in the numerous dialects which divide Europe and the world? It is one of the privileges of superior minds that they simplify their methods. And that he makes with seven notes that which was made with twenty-four, twenty-six, or even thirty-seven letters as in the Russian language, is certainly an improvement of the systems of existing languages.

The demonstration given by Mr. Sudre in the King's Concert Hall left nothing to be desired. Mr. Sudre had announced that his system could communicate with the aid of a musical instrument. A phrase was given, Mr. Sudre plays several notes on his violin, and a student comes to write on a blackboard the phrase that he had understood. The student and Mr. Sudre wrote the same phrase, at the same time, on two different blackboards, without the student being able to see the one of the master. Mr. Sudre transmitted with clear success several phrases with the aid of his violin. Later Mr. Sudre had transmitted a message by *clarions* and had demonstrated by this example the advantages which one could gain by the telegraphic sounds for the art of the army and navy.

Various travelers have reported on a system employed in China. They transmit orders by cannon. The French citizen Chappe has made telegraphic experiments, has equally thought to employ sound, which he employs using electricity. This attempt did not go anywhere and was abandoned.

Regarding the telegraphic method, or communication where the use of sounds have been employed, we will cite a circumstance in which the use of such means was beneficial. We read, in a history of the inquisition in Spain, of the unhappiness caused by the most rigorous silence which was prescribed in the prisons of Saint-Office. The prisoners communicated, when separated by a wall, by making little strikes with their fingers on the wall of their jail, and this communication, completely imperfect as it was, seemed to them sweet and brought them consolation. It broke the overwhelming boredom of loneliness.

If the system of Mr. Sudre stopped with the communication of sounds, and if it was complicated and required a lot of time, we would not be surprised. But Mr. Sudre made his means of communication a species of stenography and, under various points of view, Mr. Sudre has demonstrated his talents in perfecting the invention, and society owes him something for the long labor spend on that project. We wish the system of Mr. Sudre to be appreciated, and above all that a general language becomes common among men, and destroys all the little local interests which are so contrary to the happiness of humanity.

The following week, Sudre traveled to the north of England for a demonstration in York. The *York Chronicle*, of 10 September 1835, not only exhibits the astonishment which must have been common to everyone watching Sudre demonstrate his system, but reports that among the noble guests was the young lady who would become Queen Victoria.

> We announced last week that Mr. Sudre had arrived in York with the intention of giving some demonstrations of his musical language, of which he is the inventor, by means of which several persons can communicate among themselves by means of music. We have had the pleasure of attending these demonstrations and we can say that never have we been more astonished. Mr. Sudre communicated with the sounds of music with a person placed in an adjoining room and this person writes with the greatest accuracy all that has been thus dictated, and of which he could not have the slightest idea, since what Mr. Sudre sent him by musical interpretation was always the spontaneous thought of some person in the audience, communicated in writing to Mr. Sudre. We have heard the expression one time, that a violinist 'speaks with his instrument,' but this is certainly the first time we have found this instrument so eloquent and intelligible! It is impossible to give a complete and satisfying idea of the system of Mr. Sudre. It is completely unique and must be the result of many years of study and application. We sincerely wish that Mr. Sudre will be compensated for the many painful nights he must have spent in his work.
>
> If he can extend the practical use, it will be of very great importance. Monday night, Mr. Sudre had the honor to give a demonstration at the palace in the presence of the duchess of Kent, princess Victoria and the archbishop of York; everyone was charmed and surprised by the marvelous results that the genius and talent of Mr. Sudre, for whom all the society had the most flattering attention, particularly Mr. Lowther, a member of parliament who had asked for the patronage which the duchess, the princess and his grace the archbishop had accorded to this foreign scholar.

Sudre's final demonstration, on 8 December 1835, was a private one before the King and Queen of England, given in their vacation resort in Brighton. This was reported in the *Times* of London, on 17 December 1835.

> Mr. Sudre gave a preliminary talk relative to the applications of his method, after which the queen gave him in writing the following phrase,
>
> *I wish you success.*
>
> Mr. Sudre, with the aid of his violin, transmitted the sentence to his student who was in an adjoining room, and who immediately repeated it, to the great astonishment of the king and queen and the entire court. The queen continued, by writing the following phrases,
>
> *I am surprised.*
> *This invention does you much honor.*
>
> They were repeated by the student with as much precision as speed. Mr. Sudre then demonstrated the possibility of making communication possible between the deaf and the blind. For this he had his student enter, with his eyes blindfolded, and the queen wrote the following sentence:
>
> *This must be more difficult.*

When Mr. Sudre proposed to communicate thought, with the aid of the seven monosyllables of music, spoken as with the syllables of any other language, the queen wrote a sentence which was probably addressed to the student.

Do you understand well?

The king and queen expressed to Mr. Sudre their satisfaction which had come from this interesting discovery. Mr. Sudre could not help but express his surprise with the facility with which the queen had understood his method.

This was curious and amusing, especially the surprise expressed by Mr. Sudre regarding how quickly the queen understood the application of his method. Mr. Sudre seems to have cultivated the language of the court as well as that of music. This anecdote reminds us of an example of French flattery, when the celebrated actress Mlle. Bourgoin, gave her regards to George IV. This woman had the honor of dining with a very small group of society at Carleton House, where the king, to honor his guest, spoke only in French, a language he spoke with great facility and precision. A noble guest asked this lady if his majesty did not speak French well, and she said, with a surprise as flattering as that which Mr. Sudre manifested to the queen: 'What? Is it possible that his Majesty has ever spoken another language?'

A member of the French press had apparently been invited to this demonstration and his review appeared on 27 December 1835, in the *Revue et Gazette Musicale de Paris*. While this report, 'The Musical Language at the English Court,' contains much of the same information, we include it for its interesting new detail, as well as for the charming contrasting national style of writing.

We know that for several months Mr. Sudre, inventor of the musical language, has crossed the channel, accompanied by a student, the young Godard, and he has gone to see if England, where the study of foreign languages has always prospered, would be good enough to give the language of sounds and of notes legitimate and generous attention. The artists were not deceived in counting on the intelligence and esteem of the British: London had received him well, he and his student, and his idiom rang from salon to salon. Note that M. Sudre didn't know a word of English when leaving France, but for the one who found the universal language, what need does he have to learn the language of each country he comes to visit?

The proof that M. Sudre had no need to study beforehand in order to understand his neighbors, was that he had perfect understanding, from one salon to another, and he had gone gloriously to the salon of the king, William IV and queen Amélie, where all the other nobles, dignitaries and illustrious people had gathered. It was on the 8th of this month that the court was found in Brighton, in that fantastic pavilion, as much Chinese inside as out, to the surprise of anyone who had seen behind the Chinese door. The ornate boudoirs of marble and lacquer, cypress wood or laurel, decorated with vases in jasper and ivory, with gigantic dragons on the ceiling and chandeliers in flowers and lotus, are such as we find in our own aristocratic mansions.

When M. Sudre was introduced to this milieu of red and blue decorations, two bridge tables were brought in very kindly. The artist, placed three or four feet from the king and queen, addressed them in small talk, with sovereign authority, but not without an emotion or *tremolo* in his voice. After that he went to a table supplied with pens and things needed for his demonstration.

The queen wrote, with her gracious handwriting, the following phrase,

I wish you success!

The violin transmitted this to the student, placed in an adjoining room, and the student translated it immediately: a flattering murmur circulated in the noble assembly, in which the doubts had been removed. Then the queen wrote the second phrase, even more obliging than the first,

I am surprised!

The same dictation and the same translation by the other and the same murmur of approbation. The queen wrote a third phrase, with her kindness in a *crescendo*,

This invention does you great honor!

Then came a number of phrases, in English and in German, always dictated and translated with the same success.

To demonstrate the possibility of communicating between the blind and the deaf, the student was brought in blindfolded and the queen gave a phrase no doubt addressed to him,

Do you understand well?

Following this, M. Sudre proposed to demonstrate the communication of thought by means of seven monosyllables, spoken as syllables in any other language. The queen was again extremely kind to write the following phrase,

This must be even more difficult.

The king asked from time to time for explanations of the artist's method, and [Sudre] had to wait several times while the queen indicated with her fingers how to speak the mute language. The king seemed to take as much interest in the invention as in the inventor.

This royal demonstration, attended by Ernest, the Prince of Cambridge, the Prince of Hesse-Philipsthal, and many other notable personages, lasted an hour and a quarter. The master of ceremonies expressed the satisfaction of the king and queen to M. Sudre. The artist left carrying with him an autograph written in the hand of the queen and no doubt that would not be the only prize by which the munificent British would reward the noble efforts of the French artist. We hope for something else! We hope that France will not remain behind Great Britain!

Between 1838 and 1840 Sudre gave additional demonstrations of his two inventions in various parts of France, Belgium and the Netherlands.

In 1839, Sudre submitted the new Universal Musical Language, and apparently some dictionaries which he had completed, as an entry for the Volney Prize, which was being sponsored by the Institut de France. Unfortunately, by some technicality, his work did not meet the conditions of the competition, but his account of his meeting with the committee is quite interesting.

I was called before a commission of the Institute, with Jaubert, president, to discuss with them the results of my discovery. Here is what they asked me.

First they asked me if I could transmit Arabic; I answered yes and Mr. Jaubert wrote out a phrase in Arabic. I do not understand this language, therefore I could not read it, so I asked him to pronounce it. Immediately I took my violin and after playing a few notes, my student, Mlle Hugot, locked in another room, opened a door and repeated *in Arabic* the phrase which I had just transmitted to her by my violin.

The surprise was beyond any expectation.

A second demonstration, which consisted of transmission by writing, using musical symbols, another phrase in Arabic, had the same success. I can still remember that right after the translation, M. Burnouf himself took the paper that had the sentence and went to give it to Mlle Hugot. A moment later my student opened the door and gave to M. Burnouf the phrase in Arabic, which the president of the commission had written [in music symbols].

There was no need to do it again, I had convinced all minds; this honorable commission wrote me the following letter, which I am saving preciously as an authentic witness of the surprise that my method created before these savants.

Institut Royal de France
Paris April 26, 1839

Monsieur,

The commission charged with the examination of the works addressed for the prize founded by comte de Volney received the contents and the dictionaries which are related to the system which you have invented for the transmission of ideas by employing musical notes. The commission can only thank you for this communication, and is very satisfied to express how much it was surprised by the ingenuity of your method of transmission. The commission is pleased to declare that your discovery is worthy of the encouragement of the government. The commission would have been very happy to give you the annual prize if the restrictions set forth by M. de Volney would have permitted it.

The commission desires that you receive this letter, Monsieur, as a form of encouragement to continue your experimentation which has already produced such astonishing and positive results, and we hope that you will one day receive just compensation for your efforts.

Please receive our highest considerations.

Commissioners:

Members of the Académie française: Dupin, ainé, Feletz, Jay
Members of the Académie des Inscriptions et Belles-Lettres: Amédée Jaubert, Eugéne Burnouf, Reynaud
Member of the Académie des Sciences: Flourens.

Sudre now began to demonstrate his Universal Musical Language before a number of intellectual and scientific societies, beginning with the *Cercle des Arts*, in 1841, and in 1842 the *Société libre des Beaux-Arts*, which awarded him his first medal.

In 1844, Sudre presented his Universal Musical Language to the Royal Academy of Metz, whose report on his linguistic work concluded:

> It is to be hoped that this new and useful science will grow in the French soil, its first roots, and take a fixed character so that our country will be the first to profit.

In 1845, the Royal Academy of Rouen made a similar study and reported:

> M. Sudre in his invention of the Musical Language has distinguished his country, as well as the philosophers and friends of humanity.

On 15 June 1845, the *l'Athénée des Arts* finished its report on the work of Sudre and presented him with another medal.

> We believe M. Sudre has honored all of humanity, in all of its entirety, by contributing, in his research, to those which serve the human spirit and provides a new means of perfecting the sciences, literature and the arts. The invention of a Universal Language can be seen in various ways as furthering the marvelous discoveries of the century in which we live. In consequence the commission proposes to award M. Sudre its highest honor, 'La Couronne & La Médaille'
>
> Commissioners:
>
> Dr. Genest, president
> Paillet de Plombières
> P.-B. Fournier
> Désarnaud
> Caron P.
> Mathieu
> Doré

By 1850, Sudre was planning another trip to England and requested a letter of recommendation from Victor Hugo. Hugo responded with the following letter:

> On behalf of M. Sudre, the celebrated inventor of the Musical Language and the *Téléphonie*, who has been little compensated for his work until now, I call upon the sympathy of men who, in all countries, are interested in the progress of human intelligence and of the pacific conquest of civilization.
>
> Paris, June 22, 1850   Victor Hugo

As Sudre was preparing to depart for England, in 1852, he received another letter of recommendation, now from six famous composers of the Academy of Fine Arts of the Institute de France:

> We recommend to all persons who are occupied with the arts and sciences, M. Sudre, inventor of the Musical Language and the Téléphonie, who returns to England to make known there the different means of communication which have been approved by studies of many Commissions of the Institut.
>
> Paris, April 17, 1852
> Auber
> Halévy
> Adam
> Carafa
> Onslow
> Thomas

In 1854, Sudre went to Berlin, where he gave three demonstrations in the great Concert Hall of the king. Alexander von Humboldt attended and wrote several letters of congratulations, the last one ending as follows:

> I wanted to rush to transmit to you the news in repeating the expression of admiration which is due to you for your powerful and inventive talent.
>
> Alexander von Humboldt   November 20, 1854

In 1855, Sudre was awarded 10,000 francs by the Exposition universelle in Paris for his work in linguistics. This was a special award, available to the jury under Article 10 of their rules. The article read,

> The Jury can decide independently on the recompenses, reserving for itself, over the recommendation of the presidents and vice-presidents of the 27 first classes, to give special marks of gratitude to those participants who have been designated for their outstanding service to civilization, humanity, the sciences and the arts.

In 1856, Sudre submitted to the Academy of Fine Arts an account of the improvements he had made in his system. The Academy, after examining them, addressed to the Minister of State a report, written by the famous composer Halévy, which concluded,

> The Academy in having made know to Your Excellence the success of these tests has the honor to recommend M. Sudre to your highest benevolence.
>
> Halévy

On 17 July 1857, Sudre and his wife were invited to Plombières to have tea with the Emperor of France. As soon as they arrived, his majesty begged Sudre to make known to him the results of the Musical Language and the *Téléphonie*. After a brief explanation of the different means of communication that can be offered by seven notes of music, Sudre invited his majesty to write any phrase in French. The Emperor wrote,

> *The first who became king was first a fortunate soldier.*

Following this, Sudre took out his violin and had barely played a few notes when his wife repeated [orally] the phrase. The surprise and astonishment which this test provoked were such that his majesty exclaimed, 'It's inconceivable, it's incredible!'

The second test consisted of saying the seven notes instead of playing them on the violin. The Emperor wrote the following phrase,

> *Plombières is a charming town this evening.*

Sudre pronounced the names of several notes of music and his wife immediately repeated this phrase without hesitation in French. The same astonishment was exclaimed by his majesty and by the persons of the court who attended this brilliant evening. This demonstration lasted more than an hour and after all the tests obtained the same success, his majesty expressed his high satisfaction with Sudre.

During 1858–1861 Sudre and his wife traveled all summer to Baden-Baden, Strasbourg, Geneva, Toulouse, Bordeaux and various other French towns giving public demonstrations of the Musical Language and the *Téléphonie*, and again the local newspapers responded with praise.

In 1862 Sudre again traveled to England, to present his Universal Musical Language, together with eight dictionaries, to the Exhibition of London. Here he was awarded the Medal of Honor. The official report of the Universal Musical Language read:

> Classe 16 - Chapter VI
> Universal Language
>
> Mr. Sudre, the inventor of the *Téléphonie* and the *Universal Musical Language*, had been authorized by us to submit his system of universal language founded on music.
>
> The language of M. Sudre represents that which is common to all languages: ideas and the combinations of words borrowed from the common scale of all civilized peoples. Each idea, and its inversion, is marked by a succession of notes, and their inversion.
>
> Example
>
> 'Going up,' *sol, la, si* — 'going down,' *si, la, sol*. Each idea, represented by a group of notes, could be transmitted by the sound of the voice, by writing in the usual means of notation or by the aid of hand signs which represent them. This last way presents the means of communication among the deaf, the mute and the blind, which Nature has left with the same sense, touch.
>
> The remarkable project of Mr. Sudre, in which the proof always seemed surprising to all that have been witnesses, which has been sanctioned by the leaders of science — will it ever receive a useful application? And its author, already quite old, will he receive no other recompense other than the unanimous admiration of an unprofitable jury?

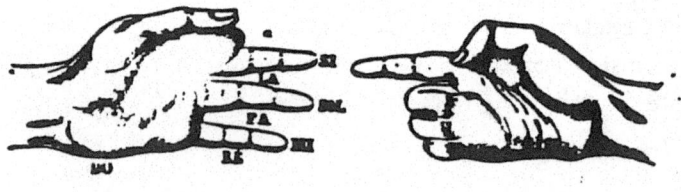

After the Death of Sudre

In 1862, after having received the *Médaille d'honneur* at an Exposition in Paris, Sudre died on 2 October. In honor of Sudre's forty-five years of devotion to the research and realization of his inventions, the poet Daveau composed the following epitaph:

> The Universal Language proclaiming your name,
> In the midst of battle makes the cannon speak.
> Your signals on the sea, sign-posts in space,
> Makes lightening shoot forth where your words pass;
> Its useful progress which traverses the night,
> From shore to shore carrying your spirit.
> Lighted in an instant, reflecting your glory,
> You transform the earth into a great conservatory,
> Or better, you're a magician, with baton in hand,
> You give the signal to the entire human race.
> You spread your art, it traverses the waves,
> Awakening echoes by the shores of two worlds.
> All respond to the call of your hand, to your voice:
> The blind understand by the touch of your fingers;
> The mute, in turn, according to your school,
> By the same touch find words.
> Also we can say: over the earth, in all places,
> The Universal Language is the language of God.

After the death of Sudre, his wife, Joséphine, devoted herself for several years to making copies and publishing the syntax and dictionaries of the Universal Musical Language, as well as continuing on her own to give public demonstrations.

She trained a student, Mlle Berthe Deprêtini, and on 1 May 1864, gave a public demonstration in the Herz Hall in Paris. The Universal Musical Language was received with unanimous praise and a number of newspapers wrote of the demonstration in the most flattering terms. Guadet, the head of the Institute for young blind persons, wrote a booklet on the potential of Sudre's system, in which observed,

> The advantages of the Musical Language of Sudre are incontestable, they are immense, but there is but one means of launching this universal language and the advantages it could produce: a government needs to become the patron. Naturally, I would prefer that it be the French government. Too often major discoveries are not recognized at home, but are carried away by foreigners, who, appreciating them better, give to their home lands the credit; that this happens should teach us something. I would like, then, for the French government to create in Paris a public school, or at least a public course, where all French could be admitted, as well as foreigners. Three months of study should suffice: or maybe make it six if you would like. I ask for an elementary course of three months to explain the theory and a course of another three months to practice the application, where we would

speak only the musical language. Each would leave the course having, in addition to his maternal language, the universal language. Soon, I have no doubt, the language of Sudre could be spoken and understood from one side of the world to the other. Soon it would be taught, I believe, in all the important schools of the world and France would be part of this new light spread over the universe. But this cheerful result can not happen unless made possible by the government.

J. Guadet, author of *Girondins*

Shortly after this she invited to her house representatives of all the scientific and literary journals of Paris for another demonstration. They all expressed the same wish, to see the Universal Language become a general communication, the bridge between nations.

One of the newspaper men attending, a M. de Léris, concluded one of his articles in the *Grand Journal* of 12 February 1865, as follows:

Why doesn't the government take care of this? Why is it that in every establishment of public instruction we don't create a course in the Universal Musical Language to compliment education? In that case we could jump over the barriers, so that people could fraternize by thought, in the best sense of the word, and the modern genius, spreading its wings, could fly from one pole to the other, without fetters, free and strong.

In the spring of 1865, a European Congress was meeting in Paris to investigate the construction of a European telegraph exchange. With the help of a deputy in the Assembly, Mme Sudre was invited to meet M. le Vicomte de Vougy, Director of the Telegraph Lines. He, in turn, sent several electric telegraphic apparatus to her home for her to experiment with the possibility of demonstrating the Universal Musical Language by telegraph. She writes that after five or six days she had mastered the problem.

On 22 March she received an invitation from the Minister of the Interior to demonstrate the possibilities of combining the Universal Musical Language with the electric telegraph before the European Congress. Here is her description of this demonstration.

The next day my student and I were in the presence of the European Congress. After having explained to those gentlemen the advantages offered by the Universal Musical Language to the electric telegraph, I begged them to write out some trial phrases.

Here are some of the ones they wrote:

I admire your perseverance.
France is the Mother of Progress.
I firmly support the success of this marvelous conception.
I am astonished.
I find this discovery marvelous.

A great number of phrases were given and again interpreted with exact fidelity by Mlle Deprêtini, my student, who in this case translated into the electrical apparatus through the keyboard which gave the seven notes of music.

After having transmitted several quick terms of the Stock Market, fractions, etc., I presented the gentlemen a *Vocabulary of Useful Phrases*, from which I could dictate to my student by pronouncing only *four notes* for each phrase.

We chose this,

Would you like to come take some tea?

'Do, si, fa, sol,' I told my student, and she repeated, 'Would you like to come take some tea?'

One of the members of the Congress doubted the possibility of this transmission and asked me if he could please write a combination of four notes and if it would be possible for me to tell him the corresponding phrase in French before I gave it to my student.

'Perfectly' I told him and he wrote at random the four notes, 're, me, sol, fa.'

Monsieur, I told him, those four notes are significant: 'Would you please be careful in the Antichamber.' Now would you please present that to my student.

So we had Mlle Deprêtini come in and Monsieur pronounced it, 're, me, sol, fa.' She also responded, 'Would you please be careful in the Antichamber.'

That was one of the tests which could carry the convictions of all minds.

I retired soon after to receive the congratulations of all parties.

Perhaps feeling she had not made her case for the Universal Musical Language, a few days later Mme Sudre wrote a heart-felt plea to the members of the Congress.

To the Gentlemen Members of the European Congress of Electric Telegraph:

Messieurs,

You will soon leave France. Paris has left you souvenirs; but there is one I would like to fix in your memory, and that is the demonstration of the Universal Musical Language, which I had the honor of performing in your presence.

You have all expressed a feeling of interest, of surprise and satisfaction that I can not forget.

You have all understood the importance and usefulness of this discovery, and many of you have manifested your opinions in phrases which I have carefully conserved.

The Universal Musical Language is destined to render the electric telegraph the most eminent service; besides transmitting the message with the greatest possible speed is the first condition of your study.

Ah! Well! The Universal Musical Language surpasses in speed all the means used up to today.

In order to communicate, from one frontier to another, you employ the letters which serve to compose words; these words are usually long, in general, and there are many in French, English and German which surpass 12 or 15 letters. On the other hand, the letters need the indication of *émissions* and *interruptions* in the [electrical] current, and the largest numbers of your letters need 3 or 4 of these emissions.

By the Universal Musical Language the most complicated words, the most abstract ideas never exist in more than four notes, and often three.

For example, I choose two of the longest words in the French Language:

Incomparablement, which would be *do, la, si*.
Constitutionnellement, which would be *si, re, la, si*.

In all languages there exist a great number of often used words which in the Universal Musical Language are represented by only 2 or 3 notes. In addition to this extreme simplicity and clarity of the transmission, think of the immense advantage of an *universal* system of symbols which could carry, from pole to pole, and which would be understood in all countries in the same manner.

> I have the honor to tell you, Messieurs, and I tell you again: five or six months at most would suffice to understand this language and to make possible the transmission of all messages and without the necessity of translators. 'The triumph of useful ideas,' Benjamin Constant once said, 'is always a question of time.'
> Confident in this thought, and also confident that the future will include this discovery, I await the passage of time and in the support of men of the most elite success, in which it is right to hope.
> I don't know if God will permit me to live long enough to see the day of the triumph of the ideas of M. Sudre, but that which I feel is the honorable vote accorded by the work of men whose spirit and talents are all of one authority, and it is already for me the highest of compensations.
> Would you agree, Messieurs, that the expression of my sentiments are the most distinguished.
>
> Paris April 4, 1865   At your wish, Joséphine Sudre

On 9 April, the following month, Mme Sudre organized a private demonstration in her home. She invited M. Louis Jourdan, after telling him of her success with the European Congress, and he responded,

> I thank you for the communication you have sent me. I would be happy to call to the new attention of the public the admirable discovery of your husband and of your indefatigable zeal to propagate it.
> I can not attend your demonstration on the 9th of April, but I will send my friends, and I am certain that, like myself, they will come back enmarveled.
> My most profound respect.
>
> Louis Jourdan

On 14 November 1865, Mme Sudre gave a private demonstration of the Universal Musical Language in the presence of the Philosophical Society. M. Poisle-Desgranges, one of the members, was asked to make a report on the work of M. Sudre and he concluded by calling for the Society to host a public discussion and demonstration.

> In summary, the linguistic work of Sudre has obtained the vote of nineteen official commissions. A funeral monument was erected in 1863 by the inhabitants of the village of d'Alby, Tarn (the village of his birth), to perpetuate the memory of this honorable man, laboriously and eminently learned.
> Now that we know what it can produce by its munificence effects, the science of the Universal Language, let me not hesitate to propose to the Philosophical Society, which has so many savants and very distinguished grammarians, and which is one of the oldest and most honored societies of France, please, because you are friends of progress of literature, of science and the arts, encourage in your next public meeting to take up the development of this Universal Language, which is called to render important services to humanity and to civilization.
>
> October 12, 1865   Poisle-Degranges.

This proposition, being accepted by the Philosophical Society, the lecture took place in a public meeting on Sunday 19 November 1865 in the Saint-Jean Hall, of the Hôtel-de-Ville.

Her final two demonstrations were on 21 December 1865, in the Bonaparte Hall, during one of the conferences of abbé Moigno, and on 22 February 1866, in the Valentino Hall, during one of the meetings of the 'men of letters.' Again, these demonstrations were carried out with great success.

In 1866, Mme Sudre published the Syntax and various dictionaries. To this publication, which appears to have been her last effort on behalf of her husband, she appended her final wish:

> So as we have come to see, the work of M. Sudre has always been crowned by the vote of competent men called to judge it.
>
> It should unmistakably carry the desired results and the desire, to furnish the various peoples of the world with a general language of communication, desired for so long a time.
>
> What a magnificent spectacle it would be if the civilized world could unite in an empire of a common language and in going through foreign countries to hear, in the murmur of the ears, the accents of a compatriot or those of a brother!
>
> In waiting for the heads of the various countries to adopt the Universal Musical Language and all the means of instruction at its disposal, I have come to tell men of intelligence and of heart that which reigns sovereign in the thought: Assist me all that you can; use your influence, so that music, which is one for all, will be able to become, through its linguistic application, the bond tying together all nations!
>
> Joséphine Sudre

About the Author

Dr. David Whitwell is a graduate ('with distinction') of the University of Michigan and the Catholic University of America, Washington DC (PhD, Musicology, Distinguished Alumni Award, 2000) and has studied conducting with Eugene Ormandy and at the Akademie für Musik, Vienna. Prior to coming to Northridge, Dr. Whitwell participated in concerts throughout the United States and Asia as Associate First Horn in the USAF Band and Orchestra in Washington DC, and in recitals throughout South America in cooperation with the United States State Department.

At the California State University, Northridge, which is in Los Angeles, Dr. Whitwell developed the CSUN Wind Ensemble into an ensemble of international reputation, with international tours to Europe in 1981 and 1989 and to Japan in 1984. The CSUN Wind Ensemble has made professional studio recordings for BBC (London), the Köln Westdeutscher Rundfunk (Germany), NOS National Radio (The Netherlands), Zürich Radio (Switzerland), the Television Broadcasting System (Japan) as well as for the United States State Department for broadcast on its 'Voice of America' program. The CSUN Wind Ensemble's recording with the Mirecourt Trio in 1982 was named the 'Record of the Year' by The Village Voice. Composers who have guest conducted Whitwell's ensembles include Aaron Copland, Ernest Krenek, Alan Hovhaness, Morton Gould, Karel Husa, Frank Erickson and Vaclav Nelhybel.

Dr. Whitwell has been a guest professor in 100 different universities and conservatories throughout the United States and in 23 foreign countries (most recently in China, in an elite school housed in the Forbidden City). Guest conducting experiences have included the Philadelphia Orchestra, Seattle Symphony Orchestra, the Czech Radio Orchestras of Brno and Bratislava, The National Youth Orchestra of Israel, as well as resident wind ensembles in Russia, Israel, Austria, Switzerland, Germany, England, Wales, The Netherlands, Portugal, Peru, Korea, Japan, Taiwan, Canada and the United States.

He is a past president of the College Band Directors National Association, a member of the Prasidium of the International Society for the Promotion of Band Music, and was a member of the founding board of directors of the World Association for Symphonic Bands and Ensembles (WASBE). In 1964 he was made an honorary life member of Kappa Kappa Psi, a national professional music fraternity. In September, 2001, he was a delegate to the UNESCO Conference on Global Music in Tokyo. He has been knighted by sovereign organizations in France, Portugal and Scotland and has been awarded the gold medal of Kerkrade, The Netherlands, and the silver medal of Wangen, Germany, the highest honor given wind conductors in the United States, the medal of the Academy of Wind and Percussion Arts (National Band Association) and the highest honor given wind conductors in Austria, the gold medal of the Austrian Band Association. He is a member of the Hall of Fame of the California Music Educators Association.

Dr. Whitwell's publications include more than 127 articles on wind literature including publications in Music and Letters (London), the London Musical Times, the Mozart-Jahrbuch (Salzburg), and 39 books, among which is his 13-volume *History and Literature of the Wind Band and Wind Ensemble* and an 8-volume series on *Aesthetics in Music*. In addition to numerous modern editions of early wind band music his original compositions include 5 symphonies.

David Whitwell was named as one of six men who have determined the course of American bands during the second half of the 20th century, in the definitive history, *The Twentieth Century American Wind Band* (Meredith Music).

A doctoral dissertation by German Gonzales (2007, Arizona State University) is dedicated to the life and conducting career of David Whitwell through the year 1977. David Whitwell is one of nine men described by Paula A. Crider in *The Conductor's Legacy* (Chicago: GIA, 2010) as 'the legendary conductors' of the 20th century.

> 'I can't imagine the 2nd half of the 20th century—without David Whitwell and what he has given to all of the rest of us.' Frederick Fennell (1993)

www.ingramcontent.com/pod-product-compliance
Lightning Source LLC
Chambersburg PA
CBHW080455170426
43196CB00016B/2821